# CHILD SCHOOLING
## IN
# INDIA

# CHILD SCHOOLING IN INDIA

*Edited by*
Pankaj Das

SHIPRA

ISBN: 978-81-7541-648-2

First Published in India in 2012

*Child Schooling in India*



*Published by*:
**SHIPRA PUBLICATIONS**
LG 18-19, Pankaj Central Market,
I.P. Ext., Patparganj, Delhi-110092
Ph. 91-11-22235152, 22236152

**Br. Off:** 4617/18, Ansari Road, Daryaganj,
Delhi-110002; Ph. 65946453, 9810522367
Email: info@shiprapublications.com
www.shiprapublications.com

# Foreword

It is indeed very heartening to see an anthology which focuses on 'Child Schooling in India'. Issues related to children and their schooling has been the subjects of considerable academic debate and discussion since several decades. Many insights have emerged through this process. What seems to be a clear pattern in the Indian socio cultural milieu is the fact that a single uniform view that defines and determines the schooling processes and experiences of children is not valid. In reality it is the psycho-social landscape which subsumes factors of caste, class, religion, region and gender that plays a major role in influencing the nature of schooling that children are likely to experience. Children's schooling experience is also dependent on the perceptions, views, beliefs and ideas that different stakeholder groups hold about what the goals and objectives of schooling are. In the contemporary context, the focus is on the holistic development of children, infusing a sense of identity in them and developing life skills that will prepare them for their adult lives. Schools are thus seen as captive preparatory spaces and as microcosms of the larger world.

It is very reassuring to see that the spectrum of articles included in this anthology relate to many of these issues. They capture different regional contexts, stakeholder groups and aspects of children's schooling. Many of them are based on primary data sources and carry very meaningful descriptions and analysis of a range of issues. They help to build perspective and enhance the readers' understanding. Usually it is very difficult to track Indian studies which provide data and conceptual understanding on the diversity that characterizes children's schooling in India. This anthology is a remarkable initiative in this direction.

While reading the studies and papers in this anthology, I was struck by the enormity of learning that took place in me. Whether it was Manipur or Jharkhand or Dang or Bundelkhand that I was interested in, there was an article for me to read. Likewise whether it was policy issues, inclusion, children in special contexts or tribal communities that I was looking for, I found articles of relevance. The width and scope of coverage of issues related to child schooling in India is remarkable. I would like to compliment Pankaj Das on this initiative. His efforts will help to enlighten a number of persons.

I wish the anthology much success and widespread outreach.

**Namita Ranganathan**
Professor, Department of Education,
University of Delhi.

# Preface

At most times in history and in most parts of the world, the age from six to fourteen years of life has been seen as the most important phase of living. Ideally, during this period, children learn how to take part in the world of activities, and how to contribute creatively, imaginatively, sensitively and reflectively to the world of activities. This period is considered as one of the hallmarks of the process of human development in many dimensions. In this stage of life, the education of the child continues in the elementary/basic schools, and for the reason this stage is called child schooling stage. Child schooling creates the base for the holistic development of the individuals as well as the total development of the country in many ways. The history of child schooling in India has been passed through many ups and downs over a period of times since independence in consonance with the changing political economy of the state.

However, child schooling in India is altogether has different meanings across gender, caste, class, region and tribes and different socio-religious communities. There is no universal definition for child schooling in India based on these parameters. For instance, the schooling for a tribal child has acquired a different experience than the schooling of a Scheduled Caste child. There are sizeable chunks of tribal child population in rural and hilly areas struggling daily to have access to the facilities of schooling in the pretext of non availability of schools, inadequate physical space, absence of innovative and encouraging pedagogical practices within the classrooms, use of alien foreign language and inappropriate medium of instructions, indifferent attitudes of the non-tribal teachers, etc. Even within and among different castes or tribes the schooling has different impact and experiences for the child. Further, schooling for the girl child in rural India is totally having different meaning and experience from the schooling of urban girl child. There are many studies across the country which have unequivocally established the fact that schooling is least preferred option for the rural girls in the socio-cultural milieu of rural society in comparison to boys and their urban counterparts. Moreover, the schooling of a dalit/ tribal/backward community's girl has told altogether different story. The experiences of the slum learners in the government schools sometimes reveal many hidden facts of child schooling in comparison to the all learners in general in the government schools in the same urban locality. Similarly the schooling of an average student is different than the schooling of an under-achiever or children with special needs. In this context one can see schooling has acquired a broader concept. Thus, the idea of schooling has diversified meanings and connotations than the usual and pre-existed universal definition of child schooling in India.

Against this intention and context just to disseminate intellectual discourse through, collecting the theoretical and empirical papers from different scholars and academicians from the different parts of the country on different issues and dimensions related to common theme of child schooling in India, the present edited volume would definitely provide a broader understanding of the concept of child schooling, its issues and challenges in present India.

**Pankaj Das**

# Contents

# 1

# Engagement of Critical Literacy and Pedagogy of Social Liberation

## *An Agenda in Schooling India*

***Pankaj Das***

The high literacy rate of a country is one of the strong indicators of national development. While the contemporary educational discourse in India has been largely involved in defining the concept of literate, as for example for the purpose of census 2011, a person aged seven and above, who can both read and write with understanding in any language, is treated as literate but a person, who can only read but cannot write is not literate. The issue of significantly improving the quality of what is taught inside and outside the schools has received less attention in the contemporary educational discourse. We are simply not aware that the literacy figure in India is not a very significant one; including the vast majority of our parents are still illiterates. Two decades of research has established unequivocally that basic education is very positively correlated with the literacy rate in the country. If children do not have access to basic skills at a very rudimentary stage then how could we imagine having the remarkable literacy rate in the country? Most children complete five years of schooling in our government schools acquiring very limited literacy and numeracy skills. Thus, the entire school education in our country is failing miserably in one of the principal goals of education- to help students understand what is learnt, relate it to the world outside the classroom and to think critically to make them better future citizens. Nevertheless, the pedagogical practices of our schooling system is revolved around the concept of rote learning rather than pedagogy of critical thinking, student-centred, democratic discourse, dialogue, empowerment and liberation, etc. as propounded by the great educationists and theorists starting from Paulo Freire, Ivan Illich, John Dewey to Mahatma Gandhi. In this conjecture, many questions are raised as what does education really mean for the masses? How the pedagogy works in our school system? How much critical pedagogy is relevant to the concept of social liberation of the child? Basing on the underling theoretical premises of "social constructivism" of Vygotsky and "pedagogy of oppressed" as propounded by Paulo Freire, the present paper is an attempt to critically analyze the concept of engagement of critical literacy in order to achieve the pedagogy of social liberation in *National Curriculum Framework –2005* in order to laid down the foundation in achieving the mass literacy in India.

## Concept of Critical Pedagogy in the Socio-psychological Perspectives

It is generally believed that education brings upliftment of the child in every realm of his/her life. This is also clearly reflected in the tenets of Hindu belief that education brings someone from darkness to light *(Sa Vidya Ya Vimuktaye)*. However, an unclear and perennial question is *what education is educating*. No doubt, out of many social and philosophical prescriptions, the basic aim of education is that the child can make a sense of life and consequently develop his/her potential which is concretized by the pedagogical practices. In a narrow sense pedagogy is defined as the art and science of teaching. It determines how a teacher thinks and acts in a formal set-up which affects students' lives and expectations. But it is a more inclusive and complex term. In the words of Henry Giroux (1997) who defines pedagogy in a broader perspective. In his own words he attempts to give a connotation as "pedagogy is not defined as simply something that goes on in schools. On the contrary, it is posited as central to any political practice that takes up questions of how individuals learn, how knowledge is produced, and how subject positions are constructed. In this context, pedagogical practice refers to forms of cultural production that are inextricably historical and political." Here one can see how the concept of simple pedagogical practices is transformed into critical pedagogical practices. Moreover, the concept of critical pedagogy has been derived and viewed by diversified thinkers and educationists in the domain of education. Many classical thinkers like Paulo Freire, John Dewey, Ivan Illich, John Holt Henry Giroux, and Ira Shor has defined critical pedagogy in their major works in different perspectives. For instance, Paulo Freire (1970; 78; 2005) and John Dewey and Lev Semenovich Vygotsky have defined critical pedagogy in socio-psychological perspectives, whereas other thinkers or pedagogues like Ivan Illich, Reimer and John Holt has analyzed the pedagogy of schooling in a very radical way and are known from anti schooling or de-schooling perspectives. Further the theorists like Ira Shor (1992a, 1996b), Patricia Bizzel (1996), Berlin (1996), Butler (1991, 1997), Giroux (1988), Gramsci (1971) has viewed critical pedagogy in post modern perspectives.

**Paulo Freire and Critical Pedagogy**

In academic sphere it focuses on educational theory and teaching and learning practices that are designed to raise learners' critical consciousness regarding repressive and alienating classroom practices and oppressive social conditions. Critical pedagogy is a teaching approach which attempts to carve a space for students to question and challenge domination, and the beliefs and practices that dominate. In other words, it is a theory and practice of carving critical space for students to achieve critical consciousness. In this tradition, the teacher works to lead students to question ideologies and practices considered oppressive (including those at school), and encourage liberatory collective and individual responses to the actual conditions of their own lives (Babu, 2007). In consonance with social, political movements in the western world in the late part of last century, the root of critical pedagogy dates back to critical theory of the Frankfurt School, whose influence is evident in the emancipator works of Paulo Freire, the most renowned critical educator. Nevertheless, the theoretical innovations in the field of pedagogy put forward by the Brazilian intellectual, Paulo Freire, one of the most significant thinkers on problems of education in the 20th Century. By raising the notion of dialogical exchange between the teacher and the student so necessary for the culture of libratory practise and denouncing of a culture of silence and oppression, Freire heavily endorses students' ability to think critically about their education situation; this way of thinking allows them to recognize connections between their individual problems and experiences and the social contexts in which they are embedded (Alan, 2003; 126). The innovative and the potential concepts like "Dialectics", "Empowerment", and "Praxis", "Conscientization", "Dialogue" are the most fundamental to his thesis of social liberation. His concern with conversation, encounter, and ethical education has strong similarities with Martin Buber's approach. Interrogation of the nature of one's social and historical situation or the critical examination of social construction, according to these two thinkers, is the single most important task for a student in whom the critical faculties are allowed to freely develop.

The teaching-learning process in the formal setting of the classroom according to Freire (1970) understanding an exercise in the development of critical consciousness (conscientization) that, apart from reflecting on important issues, gears students to take action; the teacher and the taught "both participate in the meaning making". According to Freire (1973), an adherence to conformist pedagogy only hinders the dialogical process as well as the appropriate introduction of innovative pedagogical techniques. Critical pedagogy, in opposition to conformist pedagogy, works for the development of critical consciousness of learners.

Criticizing the autocratic nature of the teacher's authority in the class, Freire (1973) argues that teaching implies working together, rather than simply talking down to the students. Excessive education, Paulo Freire (1970) argues, involves unilateralism or "banking"- the teacher making "deposits" in the taught. In the banking concept of education, teachers treat themselves as knowledgeable and bestow some kind of knowledge to the students whom they treat as completely ignorant. Jean Paul Sartre (1978) calls it's the 'digestive' or 'nutritive' concept of education. This concept negates humanization because it works on the principle of the oppressor and the oppressed and evidently such students are given to adapting to the social situation in whatever form it appears before them. The solution lies in critical pedagogy through dialogue between the oppressors and the oppressed. Dialogue in the academe becomes a civilizing and a humanizing agency of beneficial social consciousness, thereby enhancing the idea of community and justice with wider social concerns and effects. But this does not mean reducing pedagogy to a mere theory or reflection.

Informed action becomes the ultimate aim of all teaching and learning processes more relevant to the "*pedagogy of the oppressed*" or "*pedagogy of hope*" (Freire, 1970a; 1978b). This implies concern with "conscientization" or in other words, "developing consciousness, but consciousness that is understood to have power to transform reality"

BOX-1

**Freire's Method of Literary Training**

***Step 1:*** *The educators observe the participants in order to 'line in' to the universe of their vocabulary.*

***Step 2:*** *An attempt to search for generative words and themes takes place at two levels; Syllabic richness and high degree of experimental involvement.*

***Step 3:*** *A first codification of these words into visual images, which stimulated people 'submerged' in the culture of silence to 'emerge' as conscious markers of their own culture.*

***Step 4:*** *The de-codification of the generative words and themes by a 'culture circle' under the self-effacing stimuli of a coordinator who is not a 'teacher' in the conventional sense, but who has become an educator-educatee in dialogue with educatees-educators.*

***Step 5:*** *A new codification or re-codification, which is explicitly critical and aimed at action, wherein those who were formally illiterate now began to reject their role as mere 'objects' in nature and social history. They undertake to become 'subjects' of their own destiny.*

*Source*: Gerhardt 1997: 445

(Freire, 1970; 78). Freire's basic assumption was "that man's ontological vocation (as he call its) is to be a subject who acts upon and transform his world, and doing so moves towards ever new possibilities of fuller and richer life individually and collectively" (Shaull 1972;12). The Freire's (1994) critical literacy in his pedagogy of the oppressed follows the steps of construction, deconstruction and reconstruction of the objective world into subjective world. The details and the systematic steps of Freire's literacy training are given in the box-1.

**Vygotsky and Critical Pedagogy**

However, the critical consciousness will only be executed when the initial years of learning and development of the child is embedded in the social contexts as propounded by many psychological theories of learning. In this regards, the social constructivist perspective in the psychological domain of child learning has a root to explain the critical thinking of the child. In fact social cognitive theories study the impact of social factors on individuals learning. The perspective of social constructivism on child learning points out a wide range of social processes , such as cultural and historical factors, and focus on co-construction of knowledge that occur between people, not just within them. As Vygotsky (1978) argued "It is through others that we develop into ourselves". What is important in his theory is the relationship between learning and the child's social and cultural worlds. In other words, Vygotsky believes that social interactions, cultural tools and activity shape individual development and learning. Moreover, Vygotsky's theoretical perspective relies heavily on social interactions and the cultural contexts to explain critical thinking. Despite the fact that Vygotsky a social constructivist, his theory of learning gives us a way to consider both the psychological and social. He bridges both camps. For example, Vygotsky's concept of the zone of proximal development – the area where a child can solve a problem with the help (scaffolding) of an adult or more able peer- has been called a place where culture and cognition create each other (Cole, 1985). Culture creates cognition when the adult uses tools and practices from the culture (language, maps, computers, or music) to steer the child toward goals the culture values (reading, writing, weaving, and dancing). Cognition creates culture as the adult and child together generate new practices and problem solutions to add to the cultural group's repertoire (Serpell, 1993).

Thus, the theoretical basis of problem posing as a framework for critical pedagogy rests in the Vygotskian notion of *Zone of Proximal Development (ZPD)*. It is reasonable to assume that the word learner can be substituted for Vygotsky's child when one considers the varying conceptual abilities of members of any learning community Vygotsky (1986) believes that "thought and speech turn out to be the key to the nature of human con-sciousness". Further, one can draw the lines that child thinking as a *process of enculturation* is implicitly emphasized in Vygotsky's theory of learning. Enculturation is a broad and complex process of acquiring knowledge. Just as our home culture taught us lessons about the use of language, the culture of a classroom can teach lessons about thinking by giving us models of good thinking; providing direct instruction in thinking processes; and encouraging practice of those thinking processes through interactions with others.

In a nutshell, we can say that according to social constructivism approach of Vygotsky's theory that knowledge is constructed based on social interactions and experience. Knowledge reflects the outside world as filtered through and influenced by culture, language, beliefs, models, and coaching as well as the individual's prior knowledge, beliefs, and thinking affect learning.

## Critical Literacy in National Curriculum Framework-2005

The recent *National Curriculum Framework for School Education-2005* is based on the constitutional vision of India as a secular, egalitarian, pluralistic society founded on the values of social justice and equality. The aims of education are identified within this broad framework. More or less, its vision is not limited to reducing the content of education. The document implicitly reflects a deep understanding of the traditional values, cultures and socio-psycho structures of Indian society what constitutes India today. Moreover the document is fixed in such a way to act as an important tool of social change in Indian society. However, one can raise the question that does the document has the potentiality to set the agenda for social transformation and social liberation? To get the answers to this query, it is better to critically see the major principles underlined in NCF-2005.

There are essentially five guiding principles that are proposed in the NCF 2005 document. Out of which first two recommend *connecting knowledge to life outside the school* which means incorporating the experiences of the child to the teaching- learning discourse. Another principle ensures that *the learning shifts away from the rote methods* which are often practiced in the daily classroom discourse. Another quintessential feature of NCF is its *Constructivist approach* to teaching-learning. Its central tenet can be defined in terms of the proposition that knowledge does not exist independently of the subjects who seek it, and in this sense it constitutes a human construction recognizing the active capacity of the cognizing subject. Thus, it is pertinent to critically examine the concept of critical pedagogy in the NCF-2005 in the light of "Social Constructivist" and Freire's "Pedagogy of the Social liberation" perspectives against the vast socio-cultural contexts of Indian education system.

The national curriculum for schools is essentially a social document, which states not only the directions that teaching- learning process, syllabus, textbooks, evaluation and school design will have to take place, but also the basic social objectives placed in a given context.ie. *Mass literacy*. India is a pluralistic as well as the multicultural society with different religious, caste, gender and economic divergences and contradictions.

Taking cognizance of the complex social processes in India will have profound implications for the suggested learning and teaching process of mass literacy. Thus, much emphasis was given to engage in detail with the underpinnings and implications of "child-centred" education in NCF-2005. "Child-centred" pedagogy implies giving primacy to children's experiences, their voices, and their active participation. If we accept that the child coming to school is not a *"tabula rasa"* (blank slate), and the teacher is not a behaviourist practitioner then this means that the complex reality that exists outside the school, into which the child is born, and which has shaped the attitudes and dispositions of the parents, neighbours, peer groups, siblings or whatever, will have to be taken into account. Echoing the Freire's principles of dialogical mode of classroom interactions, the NCF emphasizes the voices of the children, to do things, to ask questions and to pursue investigations, sharing and integrating their experiences with school knowledge rather than their ability to reproduce textual knowledge. It should be remembered that while children construct knowledge inside the classroom, they are being given values, dispositions, social codes, and even knowledge as finished products outside the classroom in the world of the adults, which they are simply asked to obey, and not ask questions. This supports "banking concept" given by Paulo Freire. In this context, it is quite observable to see the remarks of the National Focus Group on Aims of Education "Teaching should be in the conversational mode rather than in the mode of authoritarian monologue. It is in the conversational mode that the child is likely to grow in self-confidence and self-awareness and will and more easily establish connections between the teachings and his own experience". Emphasizing the *education as lived experience* embedded in the NCF 2005, Freire's point outs the classroom teaching in terms of conscentization, which is one of the main tenets of mass literacy in India. In Freireian terminology, the NCF gears students to take action; the teacher and the taught "both learn, both question, both reflect and both participate in meaning-making".

Paulo Freire theoretical base of classroom pedagogy implies that the individual to form himself rather than be formed. In Marxian terminology, one can argue that NCF talking about that it is the "social existence that determines student's consciousness rather than it is consciousness determines his/her social existence" (Aron, 1970). To this end, he proposes that educational topics or opportunities be taken from the daily experiences the individual constantly encounters and that we avoid the current educational pitfall of resorting to artificial experiences. He proposes that one problematise his own life in order to realize that he both requires and can achieve a different status. This is all more critical for the children from underprivileged backgrounds, especially girls, as the worlds they inhabit and their realities are underrepresented in the school knowledge (NCF, 2005; 23).

The principle of dialogue as defined by Paulo Friere is one of the significant aspects of critical pedagogy which helps in building critical consciousness as discussed in NCF 2005. According to Freire "dialogue in the academe becomes a civilizing and humanizing agency of beneficial social consciousness, thereby enhancing the idea of community and justice with wider social concerns and effects" (Freire, 1970; 65).

Similarly, in regards to construction of knowledge in the teaching learning process, NCF-2005 is based on the theoretical principles of Social Constructivist approach. In the constructivist perspective, learning is a process of the construction of knowledge. Learners actively construct their own knowledge by connecting new ideas to existing ideas on the basis of materials or activities presented to them from the social contexts. Thus a child constructs her/his knowledge while engaged in the process of learning. Critical pedagogy encourages the social harmony by accepting and promoting the multiple views and perspectives and sensitivity to socio-cultural differences in Indian society. In this context, the NCF-2005 clearly points out that critical pedagogy 'entails the acceptance of multiple views on social issues and commitment to democratic forms and interactions'. This is important in view of the multiple contexts in which our schools function (Babu, 2007).

Similarly, the critical pedagogy in NCF-2005 emphasizes connecting school knowledge to life outside the school. This clearly implies that critical pedagogy accomplishes the social goal of education in the process of knowledge construction in classroom pedagogical practices. But here the question arises that whose knowledge and culturally defined symbols are transmitted in and through school knowledge and how can it be possible in single classroom situation? What NCF-2005 actually means to convey in its social constructivist pedagogy? In this context Babu (2007) argument is worthwhile by pointing out that critical pedagogy in NCF-2005 entails that school practices needs to be informed by a public philosophy that addresses how to construct ideological and institutional conditions in which they lived experience of empowerment for the vast majority of student becomes the defining feature of schooling.

Further, one can draw the lines that child thinking as a *process of enculturation* is implicitly emphasized in NCF-2005, as it is in Vygotsky's theory of learning. Enculturation is a broad and complex process of acquiring knowledge and understanding consistent with Vygotsky's theory of mediated learning. Just as our home culture taught us lessons about the use of language, the culture of a classroom can teach lessons about thinking by giving us *models* of good thinking; providing *direct instruction* in thinking processes; and encouraging *practice* of those thinking processes through *interactions* with others.

However it could be said that the overall underlining principles of Paulo Freire in NCF-2005 is based on progressive education in which 'oppression' as a basic variable in the model of human society that education has to deal with. More or less, the major principle of social constructivist in NCF is reflected in *constructing knowledge* from the child's socio-cultural contexts and experiences. In a broader and explicit way binding all the major perspectives of teaching-learning theories including Paulo Freire's *Pedagogy of Social Liberation* and Vygotsky's *Social Constructivism,* the NCF-2005 defines the Critical Pedagogy:

*Critical pedagogy provides an opportunity to reflect critically on issues in terms of their political, social, economic and moral aspects. It entails the acceptance of multiple views on social issues and a commitment to democratic forms of interaction. This is important in view of the multiple contexts in which our schools function. A critical framework helps children to see social issues are connected to their lives. For instance, understanding of democracy as a way of life can be chartered through a path where children reflect on how they regard others (e.g. friends, neighbours, the opposite sex, elders, etc), how they make choices (e.g. activities, play, friends, career, etc.), and how they cultivate the ability to make decisions. Likewise, issues related to human rights, caste, religion and gender can be critically reflected on by children in order to see how these issues are connected to their everyday experiences, and also how different forms of inequalities become compounded and are perpetuated. Critical pedagogy facilitates collective decision making through open discussion and by encouraging and recognising multiple views.* (NCF, 2005; p. 23)

### An Epilogue

Freire talked about the banking system of education four decades ago, but till date Indian educational system practices the same without any inhibition. It is true that our "education system is suffering from narration sickness" this system takes away all the creativity that would otherwise be basis for a transformative society.

Nothing will improve in the movement of achieving mass literacy unless we are prepared to radically change what is taught, learnt and evaluated in our classroom practices. Mostly the learning in our educational institutions starting from pre primary classes to higher secondary levels, almost the entire enterprise of teaching and learning in schools is action-less and de-reflective activity. A striking feature is that at elementary level, our children are struggling to memorize the formulas and procedures as instructed by our teachers and elders both inside and outside the schools. The most important task we need to do is, begin the task of reforming an educational system based on rote learning to one which promotes critical thinking and practical skills to bring the social transformation. For to achieve this goal, India needs to go a long way in the belief that one day we will have enormous numbers of creative thinkers and critical writers.

## REFERENCES

Aron, Raymond. (1970). *Main Currents in Sociological Thought*, Garden City: Doubleday.

Babu, B Ramesh. (2007): Schooling for Social Transformation: Need for Critical Pedagogy. *Indian Journal of Education*, Vol. XXXIII, No. 1, May. pp. 5-15.

Brooks, J. G. and Martin G. Brooks. (1999). *In Search of Understanding: The case for Constructivist Classrooms.* Association for Supervision and Curriculum Development, Alexandria, VA.

Freire, P. (1970). *Pedagogy of the Oppressed.* [trans. M.B. Ramos, 1982]. New York: Seabury Press.

Freire, P. (1973). *Education for Critical Consciousness*. Seabury, New York.

Freire, P. (1994). *Pedagogy of Hope: Reliving Pedagogy of the Oppressed.* [trans. R.R. Barr]. New York: Continuum.

Gerhardt, Heinz-Peter. (1997). "Paulo Friere". In Zaghloul Morsy (ed.). *Thinkers on Education.* Vol.2. New Delhi: UNESCO Publishing / Oxford & IBH Publishing.

Giroux, H. (1997b). *Pedagogy and the Politics of Hope: Theory, culture, and schooling*, Boulder, CO: Westview.

Illich, I. (1971). *Deschooling Society*. New York: Harper & Row.

Ira, Shor. (1992). *Empowering Education: Critical Teaching for Social Change*. Portsmouth, NH: Heinemann.

NCERT. 2005. *National Curriculum Framework – 2005*. NCERT, New Delhi.

Vygotsky, Lev S. (1978). *Mind in Society: The development of higher psychological processes*. Cambridge, MA: Harvard University Press.

Vygotsky, Lev S. (1986). *Thought and Language*. Cambridge, MA: The MIT Press.

Wertsch, James V. (1988). *Vygotsky and the social formation of mind.* Cambridge, MA: Harvard Press.

Wieder, Alan (2003): Voices from Cape Town Classrooms: Oral Histories of Teachers Who Fought Apartheid. *History of Schools and Schooling Series*, Vol. 39, New York.

# 2

# Scheduled Tribe Children in Primary Schools

## *A Socio-Political Perspective*

***Sambit Kumar Padhi***

Over the centuries, the structure of Indian society has undergone considerable change and people have been divided into various categories with respect to caste, colour and tribe. India has the single largest tribal population in the world compared to any other country with a population of 67.75 millions, constituting 8.1 per cent of the total population of the country (1991 census). According to the Census 2001 India has a tribal population of over 84 million which constitutes 8.08 per cent of its total population. There are 573 tribes in India residing at different parts of the country. The tribes dispersed all over the country differ from one another in racial traits, social organization cultural pattern, etc. Most of the tribal communities have their own dialects, most of them without script. There are, however, enclaves and groups, which have not been influenced by other languages, who can hardly understand the language of non-tribal population. This is the reason they are the most disadvantaged group in terms of educational development. One of the distinguishing features of the tribal is that majority of them live in scattered habitations located in interior, remote and inaccessible, hilly and forest areas of the country. More than 90 per cent of scheduled tribe workers are engaged in the primary sector or sector of economy related to the exploitation of the natural resources. Tribal own a rich cultural heritage of art, music and dance, etc. They have large number of social and religious festivals. The process of socialization of children in a tribal society is smooth and tension free. The tribal children are more free and indulgent with hardly any restrictions on their behaviour and freedom. In view of their socio-economic backwardness, geographical isolation and marginalization, the Constitution of India has incorporated specific provisions for promoting and safeguarding the interests for the tribal. Specifically article 46 of the constitution envisages that "The state shall promote with special care the educational and economic interests of the scheduled tribes and protect them from social injustice and all forms of exploitation." There are further provisions in articles 14 and 15 of the constitution for affirmative state actions in their favour.

## Tribal Education

Education in India has historically been the property of the few. Since educational development took place within the framework of stratified social system. It has always focused on the needs of the privileged ones. The status of education for various clientele groups is dependent upon their socio-political profile in a given society. The Indian society has over a period of time undergone a process of continuous degeneration, namely, from Varna Vyavastha to the caste system. The present day Indian society which interact within their own formations with the result that those with a high educational profile continue to be in an advantageous position and those who were disadvantaged once continue to remain so. Of these the Scheduled Castes (SC) and Scheduled Tribes (ST) form the largest part.

Education of tribal is an important task before the Government of India. Unfortunately the literacy rate of the tribal population is very low. The national literacy rate, of scheduled tribes, according to 2001 census, is 47.10 per cent, which is much lower than the national literacy rate, i.e., 64.84 per cent. Therefore an educational planning for such a vast group of individuals should aim at educating all its members in the school going age group. Education is in fact, an input not only for economic development of tribes but also for inner strength of the tribal communities. It also helps them in meeting the new challenges of life. There were 16 million ST children (10.87 million of 6-11 years and 5.12 million of 11-14 years) as on March 2001, out of the total child population in India of about 193 million in the age group of 6 to 12 years (Selected Educational Statistics – 2000-01, Government of India). Education of ST children is considered important, not only because of the Constitutional obligation but also as a crucial input for total development of tribal communities.

## Problems of Tribals' Education

The tribal education is lagging behind the general population. Not only this, the extent and pace of education has also remain slow among the tribal. The reasons for this can be categorised as external, internal and socio-economic and psychological. The external constraints are related to the problems and difficulties at the policy level, planning, implementation and at administration level. Internal constraints refer to problems related to the school system, content, curriculum, and medium of instruction, pedagogy, teacher-related problems, academic supervision and monitoring. The third set of problems related to social, economic and cultural background of tribal and the psychological problems of first generation learners.

Some of the major problems are given as under:

*Lack of adequate educational facilities*: Despite the government efforts, the tribal people are yet to have adequate educational facilities needed for the education of their children. The tribal live mostly in hilly tracts, scattered places, inaccessible areas, isolated habitations, and thus, making education available to them easily at their door steps is yet not to be fully possible. Conducive environment for pursuing education properly by all tribal children is not yet created in certain places. Statistical data indicate that provision of school is not available for many tribal children living in inaccessible areas and for nomadic tribal due to their non--availability of permanent establishment.

*Difference in outlook and work*: If an analysis is made on total tribal population, one can distinctly visualise that outlook, work culture and standard of living among tribal groups vary to a great extent. One groups of tribal live in a very inaccessible pockets who are still to feel the light of civilization and yet to reach the mainstream of society. Another group of tribal live in villages and willing to avail the opportunity of education but are not provided such facilities yet. Another group of tribal, who live with non-tribal in rural and semi-urban areas, try to accommodate themselves with others in the mainstream of society but due to poverty, lack of proper education and encouragement they could not able to come up. Another group of tribal, who have already come to higher stage, maintain a better and privileged life higher than even certain non-tribal. Although these four groups are tribal but have different outlook towards life and education. Similar type of treatment for elevation to be inappropriate since the last category of people does not need any type of special treatment.

*Language problem*: Tribal do have certain language problems. Most of the tribal speak languages in which there is no such written alphabet. Even in a locality, district or state, tribal speak various dialects. The language used in the school is completely different from their home language. As a result, tribal children face a great deal of difficulties in schools during their study. Despite enormous efforts to evolve certain tribal languages which would be convenient to many tribes, a lot of difficulties are encountered in evolving language in which scripts can be prepared and learning materials and instruction can be provided. As a result, they face difficulties in studying text materials. Language difficulty is one of the main reasons for backwardness and under achievement among tribal children.

*Indifferent attitude towards change and development*: This is an age of explosion. Lots of changes are taking place in every time and everywhere. Development has become a catch-word in a welfare state and emphasis is being laid on providing equality of opportunity and equity to the tribal. Government has been putting all efforts to strengthen the condition of tribal but some of tribal groups do not want to do away with their traditions and customs. This type of attitude remains a stumbling block in the process of their development.

*Mass poverty*: A very big slice of ST population is below poverty line. Research studies have proved that their utter poverty is due to their illiteracy, ignorance and conservativeness, although they are not idle and not indifferent to physical work. They are very reluctant to adopt modernity. Due to poor economic condition, they are not in a position to provide suitable education to their children.

*Poor and irregular attendance in school*: Enrolment, retention and achievement of ST children are quite below in percentage in comparison to other children. So the rate of wastage and stagnation is very high. Due to poverty, parents are unable to send their children to school; rather they prefer to engage them in earning activities, collecting fuel, fodder and taking care of siblings. Due to irregularity of attendance, tribal children remain backward and under-achievers and gradually they disappear from the educational scenario.

*Unattractive and uninteresting curriculum*: Tribal do have a specific culture, tradition, beliefs, way of living and doing things. Present curriculum is overloaded with too many school subjects that are not necessary and useful for them. As a result, these children do not show keen interest and love for studying the subjects. The curriculum prescribed by the School Board needs to be need based, flexible, simple and interesting and should contain the matters relevant to tribal life.

*Inadequate teaching materials*: Operation blackboard scheme enunciated by NPE (1986) and POA (1992) has been operated in all most all primary, upper primary schools of our country. Still then, some schools located in tribal pockets do not have necessary teaching materials and other accessories to attract the tribal children for study. Even if all materials are supplied, they are not effectively utilized by the teachers due to non-availability of basic facilities in the schools like electricity and etc.

*Non-availability of teachers*: Primary schools inhabited in tribal areas need teachers having the ability to speak the local dialect and have an interest in and aptitude for teaching the children in the tribal areas. But, there is quite dearth of such teachers, who can manage such situations. So, non-availability of teachers and inefficiency of teachers towards tribal dialect are the stumbling block for proper education of tribal children.

## Post-Independence Period Developments

After the attainment of Independence many changes have been noticed in various aspects of tribal life. A breakthrough in approach and policies for tribal development was conceived from the fifth five-year plan resulting in tribal sub approach that still continues. The tribal sub-plan approach while according priority for elementary education envisaged different strategies. However, for the first time comprehensive policy for tribal education 1986 followed by a programme of action with detailed strategies for implementation of the policies. This has provided a new perspective for tribal education for quantitative and qualitative improvement. Further, the revised policy of 1992 and programme of action strengthened the special policy and programmes for tribal education.

The initiation of National Policy on Education (NPE, 1986) stands as a watershed in the field of primary education in India as it has accorded high importance to the education of scheduled tribes, particularly universalisation of elementary education. Based on the NPE and POA for the first time the norms for establishing primary schools were relaxed to suit the tribal areas in order to improve access to education. This has facilitated to improve the schooling facility in tribal areas. However, in spirit of relaxation of norms many tribal localities were still without a school, as they did not fulfil even the relaxed criteria.

In a bid to improve the pace of educational growth many programmes and approaches are undertaken at the state and central level. The result of the efforts showed a growth in the literacy rate. The census of Indian for the period 1971, 1981, 1991 and 2001 provides the rate as 10.30 per cent, 16.35 per cent and 29.60, and 47.10 per cent respectively.

## Primary Education: Access and Participation

In the backdrop of different policies and programmes formulated to provide educational access in tribal areas, it is essential to examine the access condition for primary education. When we compare the access condition in between 1982-92, it is found that considerable improvement has taken place in terms of the percentage of habitations having primary schools and the coverage of population by these schools.

More importantly, a positive aspect is that the number of habitations having schools beyond 2 km is fast decreasing. In recent years expansion of primary schools helped to reduce the distance between schools and habitations particularly in case of those who had to go more than 2 km distance. In almost all the tribal concentrated states the number of schools within 1 km of the habitation has increased and higher percentage population coverage is achieved. The Sixth Survey of Education-1992 shows that 78 per cent of tribal population and 56 per cent of tribal habitations have been provided primary schools within their habitation. Another 11 per cent of tribal population and 20 per cent of their habitations had schools within the range of more than half and less than one kilometer distance. However, for 12 per cent of tribal population primary school facilities are located in more than a kilometer distance. These are the people who are scattered in small habitations with less than 100 population habitation.

When we examine the extent of availability schools for people covered under different population slabs of habitations, it is evident that more than 90 per cent of tribal population and the habitations fewer than 500 and above population slabs had access to primary schools within the habitation. The remaining primary schools were located within a half a kilometer to a kilometer distance. In case of habitations within the population range of 300 persons 76 per cent of habitations and same percentage of population in these localities were having the primary schools in their habitations. Although apparently it looks that a higher percentage of habitations in lower population slabs did not have schools in their habitations, in reality the percentage of population covered by these habitations constitute very small segment to total tribal population.

More interestingly the tribal habitations in all the categories of population slabs are in favourable placed than rural habitations in terms of having access to primary schools within the habitation. On the other hand, in the higher category of population slabs the extent of coverage of habitations by primary schools almost equal in tribal and rural areas. In other words, habitations with 500 and less population have better access to primary education in tribal areas than the rural habitation. This is due to favourable polices and relaxation of population and distance norms for establishing schools in under privileged areas. This evidently shows the role of conscious efforts though special policies in the promotion of education in tribal areas. However, in case of smaller population slabs the percentage of tribal habitations having schools located at a distance of more than 1 km is slightly higher than that of rural areas. However, this improvement is not same across all the states in India. The extent of access to primary schools in different tribal concentrated states shows an uneven spread of schooling facilities.

In view of difficult terrain, geographical and ecological barriers in tribal areas the distance of more than half a kilometer is a difficult proposition for young children to attend school. In fact the distance of one kilometer and above between the school and habitation means practically these habitation and inhabitants lack access to primary schools given the tribal context. Thus, a little more than one-fifth of total tribal population is constrained by this problem. In this context one can note that though the policies have been largely favourable to the tribal population still a large number of tribal habitations are without schools. Moreover, 10 per cent of the tribal habitations have schools beyond 2 km. In view of various geographical and ecological barriers prevalent in tribal areas the 0.5 kilometer norm at times looks a rather inflated proposition as it makes difficult to cross that distance for children during hostile weather condition.

Since the Sixth all India Educational Survey, i.e., after 1993 onwards there was considerable improvement in the front of access more particularly in tribal areas under different educational projects.

### Enrolment in Primary Schools

Education of ST children is considered important, not only because of the Constitutional obligation but also as a crucial input for total development of tribal communities. So far the enrolment of tribal children in primary schools are concerned, the data of eleven states are compiled and identified the enrolment of tribal children in comparison to other social groups. (Table 2.1). It is observed that enrolment is not quite encouraging. It can also be reported that enrolment of tribal children in primary school is 11.70 per cent compared to19.90 per cent, 42.40 per cent, 11 per cent of SCs, OBCs, and Muslims children respectively at national level.

**Table: 2.1 Primary School Enrolment of Children of Various Social Groups at in Selected States (Per cent)***

| *States* | *SC* | | *ST* | | *OBC*** | | *Muslims* | |
|---|---|---|---|---|---|---|---|---|
| | *Popula-tion* | *Enrol-ment* | *Popula-tion* | *Enrol-ment* | *Popula-tion* | *Enrol ment* | *Popula tion* | *Enrol-ment* |
| Assam | 6.90 | 9.30 | 12.40 | 14.60 | - | 23.20 | 30.90 | 35.10 |
| Bihar | 15.70 | 18.20 | 0.90 | 2.40 | - | 60.20 | 16.50 | 13.00 |
| Delhi | 16.90 | 11.00 | 0.00 | 0.40 | - | 8.70 | 11.72 | 12.30 |
| J & K | 7.60 | 8.50 | 10.90 | 15.80 | - | 8.30 | 67.00 | 66.40 |
| Jharkhand | 11.80 | 15.40 | 26.30 | 31.70 | - | 45.40 | 13.90 | 10.70 |
| Karnataka | 16.20 | 19.60 | 6.60 | 8.10 | - | 51.90 | 12.20 | 14.70 |
| Kerala | 9.80 | 11.60 | 1.10 | 2.40 | - | 63.40 | 24.70 | 26.20 |
| Maharashtra | 10.20 | 14.80 | 8.90 | 12.80 | - | 32.30 | 16.10 | 9.30 |
| UP | 21.10 | 27.10 | 0.10 | 0.60 | - | 49.90 | 18.50 | 9.60 |
| Uttarakhand | 17.90 | 26.80 | 3.00 | 3.30 | - | 25.50 | 11.90 | 13.80 |
| W Bengal | 23.00 | 27.20 | 5.50 | 6.70 | - | 4.70 | 25.30 | 28.30 |
| **India** | **16.20** | **19.90** | **8.20** | **11.70** | - | **42.40** | **13.40** | **11.00** |

*Figures compiled from (Mehta, 2011). **OBC Population is not mentioned in Census, 2001

The situation is equally dismal at upper primary stage (Table 2.2). It is observed that enrolment of tribal children in upper primary school is 9.40 per cent compared to19.20 per cent, 41.90 per cent, and 9.10 per cent of SC. OBC and Muslims children respectively at national level.

**Table 2.2: Upper Primary School Enrolment of Children for Various Social Groups in Selected States (Per cent)**

| *States* | *SC* | | *ST* | | *OBC*** | | *Muslims* | |
|---|---|---|---|---|---|---|---|---|
| | *Popula-tion* | *Enrol-ment* | *Popula-tion* | *Enrol-ment* | *Popula-tion* | *Enrol ment* | *Popula tion* | *Enrol-ment* |
| Assam | 6.90 | 10.80 | 12.40 | 16.40 | - | 26.50 | 30.90 | 25.60 |
| Bihar | 15.70 | 13.50 | 0.90 | 1.60 | - | 62.00 | 16.50 | 10.30 |
| Delhi | 16.90 | 10.50 | 0.00 | 0.30 | - | 3.10 | 11.72 | 10.70 |
| J&K | 7.60 | 8.80 | 10.90 | 11.30 | - | 8.60 | 67.00 | 64.00 |
| Jharkhand | 11.80 | 13.00 | 26.30 | 27.10 | - | 48.70 | 13.90 | 9.90 |
| Karnataka | 16.20 | 18.30 | 6.60 | 7.50 | - | 53.00 | 12.20 | 13.80 |
| Kerala | 9.80 | 11.30 | 1.10 | 2.00 | - | 61.00 | 24.70 | 22.00 |
| Maharashtra | 10.20 | 14.60 | 8.90 | 9.50 | - | 32.70 | 16.10 | 8.00 |
| UP | 21.10 | 26.50 | 0.10 | 0.50 | - | 47.00 | 18.50 | 7.50 |
| Uttarakhand | 17.90 | 24.70 | 3.00 | 3.80 | - | 18.70 | 11.90 | 7.30 |
| W Bengal | 23.00 | 27.80 | 5.50 | 5.20 | - | 8.80 | 25.30 | 20.00 |
| **India** | **16.20** | **19.20** | **8.20** | **9.40** | - | **41.90** | **13.40** | **9.10** |

*Figures compiled from (Mehta, 2011), **OBC Population is not mentioned in Census, 2001

The participation of tribal children in education is pretty low in comparison to other. Enrolment of tribal children was about 9 million in classes of I-V during the year 1997-98. However, the number of tribal children enrolled in primary classes of I-V has increased in last ten years. The increase in number of students enrolled need not necessarily be due to population growth during this period as the growth rate of enrolment is very high compared to population growth rate. More importantly, corresponding to the increased enrolment at primary stage the enrolment in middle stage had also improved in manifolds.

### Promotion Policy

Majorities of the states have automatic promotion policy at primary stage unless the required attendance and expected minimum level of competencies are fulfilled. Even after the non-detention policy in almost all the states the students are detained in the same class for more than one year. According to the Sixth all India Educational Survey between the classes I and V, 11 per cent of tribal children repeat the same class for more than one year.

More importantly the per cent of repeaters in lower classes, i.e., up to class III is higher compared to higher classes. In some of the states like Tripura, Bihar and Arunachal Pradesh nearly one-fifth of the students in class I are detained in the same class for repetition. In Madhya Pradesh, Orissa and Rajasthan also the repeaters per cent is considerably high in all classes. In some of the states though the per cent of repeaters declines in classes II and IV but their per cent increased in class V (Sujatha, 1994). There are several reasons for the repetition: poor attendance-rate, low academic performance, language problem, etc.

### Academic Performance of Tribal Students

Almost all the studies in this regard in India showed that the tribal students in primary classes have lower achievement scores compared to non-tribal population (Shukla, 1994, Govinda and Varghese, 1989, Jhangira 1993, Varghese 1993, Sujatha, 1998, Prakash, 1998). The low achievement levels among tribal were attributed to school related variables as in the case of non-tribal students. However, the tribal students had additional disadvantages arising out of social and location factors that affect their achievements levels. In other words the tribal students' performance varies among different schools irrespective of their location, family background and management type of the school (Sujatha, 1998). A silver lining in this regard is that the achievement levels of tribal children had improved from the base line study conducted under District Primary Education Programme (DPEP) in 1993 to achievement test conducted during 1998 in the same districts (Prakash, 1998).

### Recent Initiatives

Education is directly related to the development of a country. Efforts are being made both by the Union Government as well as state governments to provide numerous facilities to the disadvantaged groups with a view to bring them at par with the various advantaged groups. Opening of schools in habitations with a higher concentration of disadvantaged population, free education, merit scholarships, attendance scholarships, free uniforms, midday meals, and providing coaching classes to the needy children are some interventions which aim at increasing the enrolment and retention of Scheduled Tribe children in school. Besides there are various government and nongovernmental organizations that have also put in significant efforts of raise the educational level of the disadvantaged population.

During the past few years, tribal education has witnessed a rapid transformation particularly in the arena of access, pedagogic reform and community participation. A brief overview of these trends will provide a critical understanding of ground realities and scope for future prospects.

As has been discussed in the earlier section, much of the emphasis is given to the improvement of access in tribal areas. Along with the flexibility of norms regarding the opening of schools and prioritizing tribal areas for new schools a few innovations and strategies were adopted. Some of the recent micro-level evidences show that the several micro-level interventions and initiatives like mid day meal scheme, creation of self help women groups (SHWG), environment building programmes under different projects, establishment of Integrated Tribal Development Agencies (ITDA), appointment of local tribal teachers, developing partnership between school and village communities in school management had helped in raising awareness level among tribal to realize the importance of education and positive attitude towards girls' education (Sujatha, 1999).The establishment of non-formal schools and alternative schools in recent years further bolstered the effort towards the development of tribal education. In fact, the alternative schools and non-formal educational centres were opened with the belief that the tribal children need a different environment for education than their counterparts and therefore an alternative is a necessity rather than another means. Community schools have come up in states like Andhra Pradesh in tribal areas to provide alternative educational infrastructure to tribal children. Similarly, Educational Guarantee Scheme is another innovation at the access front.

In an effort to improve the teaching learning process some innovations were incorporated. One of such innovation is joyful learning method. This is introduced in many a tribal schools to achieve more enrolment and retention. In order to improve the academic monitoring and supervision cluster Resource centres and school complex have been formed. The resource persons do regular monitoring and provide school based training to sustain the capacity building efforts. As a result of such decentralized monitoring of teachers and teacher competency building through training has helped to break isolation among the teachers to less teacher absenteeism and better teaching capabilities.

Community participation is a major innovation in current educational development strategy. The formation of Village Education committees (VECs) to monitor and guarantee the participation of community in school activity is a step in this direction. The VEC is entrusted with certain supervisory and administrative responsibilities. Now even attempts are made to provide training to VEC members in the basics of school management and administration by which they can be more effective and involved. Under the DPEP the VECs are revitalized and in many tribal areas VECs are given the responsibility of constructing the school building.

The educational development of children belonging to the Scheduled castes and Scheduled Tribes is a special focus in the Sarva Shiksha Abhiyan. Textbooks in mother tongue were recommended for the tribal children at primary stage where they do not understand regional language. Special training for non-tribal teachers to work in tribal areas, including knowledge of tribal dialect also was emphasized. The Right to Education (RTE) which has been implemented from 1st April 2010 focus on free and compulsory education for all category of children in general and tribal children in particular. It has been felt that education has been playing a very crucial role to bring the tribal population in the mainstream of social life.

**Steps Suggested under National Policy on Education**

The National Policy on Education, 1986 (modified in 1992) lays special emphasis on the removal of disparities, between different categories of people. The Policy gives a clarion call for attending to the specific needs of those who have been denied equality so far.

The following measures will be taken urgently to bring the Scheduled Tribes at par with others:

*(i)* Priority will be accorded to opening primary schools in tribal areas. The construction of school buildings will be undertaken in these areas on a priority basis under the normal funds for education, as well as under the N.R.E.P., R.L.E.G.P., Tribal Welfare Schemes, etc.

*(ii)* The socio-cultural milieu of the STs has its distinctive characteristics including, in many cases, their own spoken languages. This underlines the need to develop the curricula and devise instructional materials in tribal languages at the initial stages, with arrangements for switching over to the regional language.

*(iii)* Educated and promising Scheduled Tribe youths will be encouraged and trained to take up teaching in tribal areas.

*(iv)* Residential schools, including Ashram schools, will be established on a large scale.

*(v)* Incentive schemes will be formulated for the Scheduled Tribes, keeping in view their special needs and life styles. Special remedial courses and other programmes to remove psycho-social impediments will be provided to improve their performance in various courses.

*(vi)* Anganwadis, Non-formal and Adult Education Centres will be opened on a priority basis in areas predominately inhabited by the Scheduled Tribes.

(*vii*) The curriculum at all stages of education will be designed to create an awareness of the rich cultural identity of the tribal people as also of their enormous creative talent.

**Future Perspectives**

First of all emphasis should be given to the quality and equity rather than quantity as it has been done in all these years. In fact quality education has no alternative and therefore, our prime focus should be on the quality.

Second, the school schedule should be prepared as per the local requirement and usages rather than uniform pattern. It has been found that vacations and holidays are with a cognizance of local contexts.

Third, the availability of locally relevant materials will not only help the children to associate those one with the school but also facilitate faster learning.

Fourth, in order to make education effective and sustainable it is essential that we should built a partnership between the community and the government to guarantee regular monitoring of the community and the government to guarantee regular monitoring of the functioning of schools effectively.

Fifth, environment building is of immense importance in the context of educational development among tribes. Community mobilization is the key to environment building; therefore, this should be given importance. Once this is achieved it should not be left in lurch but should be continued.

Sixth, skill development, competency building and motivating the teachers also need to be looked upon for sustaining educational development. Teacher should be made the centre of educational transformation and, therefore, they must remain as the primary facilitator. There should be novelty in pedagogy and curricula so that the interest and motivation of teachers remain at a higher level. This will make the teachers more competent in withering the challenges of education in future. Attempts must be made not just to select the local teachers but to find out the best among them who is competent and trained.

In fact, Scheduled Tribe students are not able to pursue their study in standard public schools due to financial burden although they are meritorious. To provide quality education to gifted ST learners and to upgrade their achievement level, pace-setting elementary schools should be established specifically for them and by making certain seats reserved for them in other standard institutions. Besides, all attempts should be tailored to suit the needs of slow and backward learners and underachieves through remedial instruction and compensatory education. They should be brought under the provision of scholarship, encouragement, hostel accommodation and dietary requirements. Both girls and boys should be given due scope for the enfoldment of their inherent potentialities. Ashram schools specifically meant for residential education of ST children should provide ample avenues of opportunity in degree and dimension to make a mark in the specialised areas of inborn ability.

Moreover, all efforts should be made through education to inculcate an understanding among teachers and students about the variety, novelty and richness of culture of ST and their contribution to Indian culture and economy. A lot is done and to be done for the education of ST population. Proper monitoring for its successful implementation is an essential requisite. A concentrated effort and sensitization of all concerned with-will and zeal to ameliorate their condition through proper education is the right remedy for many maladies.

## REFERENCES

Annamalai, E. (2001). *Managing multiculturalism in India: Political and linguistic manifestation*, New Delhi: Sage.

Das Gupta, N.K. (1959). Tribal Language and Education, *Man in India.*

Dubey, S.C. (1972).Expert Committee on Tribal Development , GOI, New Delhi

Fishman, J.A. (1999). *Hand Book of Languáge and Ethnic Identity,* New York: OUP.

GoI. (2002). *The Indian Child: A Profile.* Department of Women and Child Development, MHRD, New Delhi

Kangas, T.S. (1999). *Education of Minorities*, New York:OUP

Majumdar, D.N. (1958). *Races and Culture in India* , Bombay: Asia Publishing House

Mehta, Arun (2011). Elementary Education in India: Progress towards UEE. DISE-NUEPA, New Delhi.

National Policy on Education (1986), MHRD , GOI, New Delhi

Nehru, Jawaharlal (1954). 'Forward' to Elwin, V., Philosophy for Tribal Development, New Delhi

Patnaik, N. (1982). Tribal Life in Orissa, Souvenir Orissa Sahitya Academy, Bhubaneswar.

Ratnaih (1977). *Structural Constraints of Tribal Education*, New Delhi: Sterling Publication

Rout, P.C. (1989). Tribal Education in Orissa, Bhubaneswar: Eastern Graphics.

Sujatha, K (1994), *Educational Development Among Tribes: A Study of Sub-Plan Areas in Andhra Pradesh*, New Delhi: South Asian Publishers.

Wetzlaugk, M.S. (1985). Official Discourse, Pedagogic Practice and Tribal Education: A case study in Contradiction, *British Journal of Sociology of Education.*

# 3

# Lived Experiences of Tribal Children in the Classroom

## *An Insight from a Middle School in Jharkhand*

***Abhineet Kala Lakra***

Tribes are educationally among the most disadvantaged groups in India. Scheduled tribes have been excluded from formal education system due to their geographical isolation, ethnic and cultural differences, socio-economic differences and marginalisation by dominant mainstream society. Education of the tribes was given importance after independence but policy makers appear to have been largely concerned with the idea of 'integration' in 'mainstream' society. Concern was shown towards them by trying to bring them into the mainstream Indian society by making policies. Various policies such as National Policy on Education (1968, 1986), Programme of Action (1992), and programmes such as District Primary Education Programme (DPEP), 'Sarva Shiksh Abhiyaan' (SSA), 'Janshala' project etc. were initiated by the government with the goal to ensure a maximum level of participation of tribal children in education. The goal is to decrease the drop-out rate by reaching hundred per cent enrolment and also to improve the level of achievement among the children. The purpose behind all these has been to make basic education more accessible and effective.

Objective of the policy has largely been to bring Scheduled Tribes at par with the general population in terms of enrolment, retention and learning levels (minimum levels of learning). Though concerted efforts have been made both at central and state levels, yet the quality of education varies at inter and intra state level. The gap between Scheduled Tribes and the non-scheduled groups continue. Disparities also continue among different states and between rural and urban areas and males and females, as a result of which some states and some tribal communities fail to make progress in education, despite various incentive schemes. Why this is so?

What are the reasons for their failure to progress and for high drop outs? Why do they continue to remain backward in educational competition? Through my observations of classroom processes and tribal children's experiences (related to cultural and language differences) which still remains an area of research in order to remove the obstacles of educational mobility of tribal communities, I have tried to look into the afore mentioned questions that plague the community under study. The paper explores the manner in which school environment and practices influence and affect the educational experiences of children belonging to tribal communities. The paper argues that social relations and classroom practices are responsible for tribal child's failure other than lack of interest.

**The Context: Sithio Village**

The field study was located in the state of Jharkhand which is one of the educationally backward states in India. Scheduled tribes constitute around 26.3 per cent of the total population of the state (Census 2001). Education among the tribes is extremely poor, i.e. the literacy rate in Jharkhand in 2001 is 40.67 per cent (lower than other states), which is less than the literacy rate of Scheduled tribes across India (SES, 2007).

A village named Sithio of Senha block in Lohardaga district of Jharkhand was chosen as a site of the study. The study was conducted in a Government Middle School (established in 1906) comprising of tribal and non-tribal students and teachers. The school comprised of children coming from diverse communities having higher number of Scheduled Tribe children followed by Other Backward Classes. Field work was conducted for 45 days in the year of 2008.

Sithio village is 5-6 km away from the main town of Lohardaga. The village has a number of castes and tribal communities such as, *'Teli'*, *'Oraon'*, *'Mahli'*, *'Dhobi'*, *'Rajput'*, *'Garedi'*, *'Kumhar'*, *'Brahmin'*, *'Nai'*, *'Turi'*, *'Lohar'* and *'Lohra'* in which *'Oraon'*, *'Mahli'* and *'Lohra'* are tribes. The households are spatially dispersed and not clustered according to castes/community.

The tribes of Sithio village were mainly cultivators and agricultural labourers and are engaged in other low paid sectors. Majority of the households own small land holding with a significant percentage in the category of landless and marginal holding. They are also engaged in other occupational practices like selling vegetables, labour work, rickshaw pulling, driving, and some work under NREGA (National Rural Employment Guarantee Act) and are migrant labourers. As such, they have to survive on ₹ 800 to ₹ 3000 a month. The socio-economic condition of tribal people is poor. They suffer from poverty and irregular incomes. Almost all of them have '*kachcha*' houses. Toilet-bathroom, electricity and other facilities are lacking in their houses. The level of parental literacy is abysmally low.

## Methodology

Micro level qualitative exploration based on 'ethnographic' approach was adopted. Data was collected through in-depth interviews, informal discussions, and non-participant observations of the school (guided by the theoretical framework of 'symbolic interactionism'). Semi-structured interview schedules with open ended questions were used for teachers and children. The sample comprised of 31 children [24 tribal children (11 boys and 13 girls) and 7 non tribal students (5 boys and 2 girls)] and 10 teachers. They were purposively selected for the interview. Non-participant observations (unstructured) of two classrooms (V and VIII) were done keeping the theoretical framework of 'symbolic interactionism' (how actors interact). The objective of the research was to explore the classroom processes and tribal children's experiences. An attempt was made to study peer relations in school to understand the nature of peer relations and how they are influenced by the identity of being 'tribal'/belonging to other communities. The study also tried to observe the nature of tribal children's participation in the class.

## Theoretical Framework

The theoretical framework of 'symbolic interactionism' coined by Herbert Blumer (1937) has been used. It guided the actual process of data collection and analysis of data. The two words, 'symbols' and 'interaction' produce meaningful interaction, wherein, interaction involves giving social objects symbolic value. People interpret and act on the basis of symbols. But for Blumer (1969), the most significant feature of all human association is that the participants take each other into account as a basis of conduct.

The framework was based on Woods' (1983) interactionist approach, where I had taken five out of six main concerns, i.e. *'context', 'perspectives', 'cultures', 'strategies' and 'negotiation'*. The first concern is, a school consists of different *'contexts'* and situation, which are interpreted differently by different individuals (teacher, student, other staff). Here, the 'definition of the situation' by the individual is important in identifying the various situations. This can be seen through Goffman's (1959) 'front stage' and 'back stage'. The second concern is teacher and student *'perspectives'*, i.e. the 'framework of ideas' through which they 'construct their realities and define situation' (as cited in Woods, 1983:8). These "perspectives are based on certain assumptions which are both culturally specific and context-bound" (Ibid.). The third is that these perspectives arise out of *'cultures'*, i.e. forms of life – values, beliefs, pattern of speech, behaviour, etc., which develops when people come together for specific purpose. The fourth aspect is *'strategies'*, the way of achieving goals. Perspectives are linked to strategies. It is a central concept "for it is where individual intention and external constraint meet" (Woods, 1983: 9). Individuals especially teachers devise different strategies to cope with the situations in the school. The fifth is *'negotiation'* which is a kind of working agreement, including the "act of identifying, interpreting, reckoning, and choosing" to seek one's interests (Woods, 1983: 11). Negotiations are "often conflictual, marked by rancour, and bad feeling, not only concerned to optimize one's own concerns, but to belittle the other's" (ibid.). These aspects of social life in the school as described by Woods (1983) were examined in their relationship with one another in my presentation of the everyday lived realities of the school where interaction takes place between participants.

### Tribal Children's Schooling

Today, tribal society is rapidly changing and they can no longer be seen as unchanging 'nomadic' or 'primitive' social groups. Tribes are increasingly aware that their traditional, social and economic institutions have disintegrated while their culture and languages are being destroyed by the process of 'modernization' and 'development'. On the other hand they know the value of education and are looking toward educational institutions to offer avenues for mobility and better life chances for their children. Tribal parents of Sithio village wanted their children (both girl and boy) to be educated to eliminate oppression of the dominant group from their society. They did not want their children to work as bonded labourer like them. Parents sent their children to school which is in their vicinity to get some wisdom to survive in this world.

However, school institutions on the other hand did not help tribal children to change their educational situation. Tribal children are vulnerable in the system as their ethnic cultures and languages are excluded and not given importance in the school curriculum. Schools try to assimilate these children into mainstream culture by engaging them in the ways of the majority and also insisting that they relinquish their culture by devaluing their own culture. This could be seen in the present study of a school and classroom processes.

### Tribal Children and Classroom Processes

Classroom processes include classroom organisation, teaching learning process, teacher-students interaction, curriculum, official and hidden, peer relations and so on. Teacher and students involve in giving, receiving and sharing knowledge in the classroom. They are also, according to Delamont

(1976), responsible for negotiation in order to maintain classroom order (as cited in Shaw, 1981).

*Classroom Organisation:* The classroom organisation or seating arrangement was observed to reinforce differentiation based on gender and caste/community hierarchy. First two rows were occupied by the dominant non-tribal students, forcing tribal students to sit at the back. Due to tribal students' silence and no rotation of seats by the teacher, it had become an unspoken rule. Preferences were given to 'good' and 'bright' non tribal students, leaving tribal students to remain back benchers who were perceived as 'weak', passive and non-responding students.

*Teacher-Student Relations:* Teachers and students bring their social status and experiences in school which affects their relationship and interaction. Most teachers were seen not interacting with tribal students inside the classroom and there was a big gap between teacher-student relations. Teachers were unfriendly and unapproachable and tribal students did not converse or share their problems with teachers. Inter –cultural communication was there as a retarding factor. Tribal students' ethnic culture and languages were not seen in positive light. A non-tribal teacher (OBC) believed that,

> "tribal children are weak because of their heredity, culture and environment. Their culture does not help them to move upward in their development. During festivals they engage themselves in drinking and eating and spend their time in enjoyment. The main reason of their backwardness is that they do not use their time. Drinking is their weakness". (Teachers' interview)

Tribal students were stereotyped on the basis of their socio-cultural background for their backwardness. Some tribal children were aware of teachers' negative perceptions and stereotypes about them as 'weak' and 'dull' students (Sujatha 1996). They were aware of teachers' favouritism for those who were active and interactive in the class. For instance, one of the tribal boys (class V) reported:

> "Teachers pay attention to intelligent students only. They mostly ask questions from the front bench students (General/OBC) who are good in studies. They hardly ask questions from me as I am unable to give answers". (Children' interview)

The statement shows tribal boy's awareness of teachers' bias and the perception of himself as weak in studies. However, Woods says that the general view of students is that "teachers should be 'human', should be able to 'teach' and make you 'work' and keep control" (Woods, 1983:54). It is evident that most of the tribal students liked particular teacher for his/her "way of teaching", "explaining the lesson" and "talking nicely to them" in the class. Some teachers were disliked for "not teaching well", "scolding", "abusing", "not bothering to understand their problems" "treating harshly" and "beating". It was observed that liking for a particular subject was also dependent on who taught the subjects.

*Classroom Interaction and Pedagogy*: In the classrooms, teacher-pupil interaction is central to teaching learning processes. During the classroom transaction, classroom activities follow a strict routine where students are supposed to obey their teachers. According to Brint (1998), students are not free to move or talk and they sit in their places with their eyes upon the teachers. The classroom is teacher-centred rather than child-centred. There is no 'dialogue' as Freire (1970) opined but a kind of monologue where students are expected to listen as a passive audience.

However, according to Krishna Kumar, teachers are the 'meek dictators' in the classrooms whose, as Delpit pointed out "issues of power are enacted in classroom that is, the power of the teacher over the students" (1997: 583). The school that was observed was also not immune to these qualities of teachers.

The same conventional pedagogy of teaching (reading the text-book) was used by emphasizing on rote memorisation and repetition (see Sujatha, 1996) of poems, names of the poets/authors, facts, dates, word meanings, definitions, formulas and students were punished for failing to do so. Teachers did not bother whether students had books with them or not.

This was detrimental to all children and especially those coming from the tribal communities. The homework given by teachers (who were insensitive to home environment) was meaningless as tribal children did not get time or assistance from their family members to complete homework. Errors made by students were seen as something to be ashamed of. For instance, a tribal student of class V was scolded for not reading correctly. The Maths teacher (OBC) said:

> "... do you know to read 'ie', 'oo', 'harsi', 'dirghi', or you just pass without knowing? People climbed on the mountain, went to space, they are flying aeroplane and you don't know 'ka', 'kha', 'ga', 'gha'? People work hard and rise high and you...." (Classroom observation)

The boy had difficulty in reading due to language problem which was ignored by the teacher. Students became the brunt of teacher's anger and were ridiculed and scolded for not paying attention in the class. No activities or teaching aids were used for teaching. Students had very little opportunity to participate and were supposed to answer only when asked to do so (see Sujatha 1996). Students' home/local knowledge was not used to explain them. Even mathematics was taught without using teaching aids, insisting students to memorise use their mind and think on their own while solving the mathematics problems. For instance, students were asked to repeat loudly and memorise the definition of 'rectangle' in the class and were scolded or beaten for not doing so.

Of course this was not entirely the case with all teachers. An English language teacher believed in activity based learning and did try to engage children in learning, but here again children's imagination and creative thinking was not appreciated adequately. For instance, during English lesson in class VIII, the teacher drew the pictures of 'a tree', 'a cap', 'a man' and 'a monkey' on the blackboard and explained the meaning of these words. The teacher said,

*Teacher - "I have drawn some pictures. Now you write a story based on this picture. First you write in Hindi then we will translate it into English. I am giving you 10 minutes. Don't talk and do your own work.*

*Boy - We have to write on our own sir?*

*Teacher - Yes, all of you construct your own story.*

After 10 minutes:

*Teacher - "All of you stop writing. Ramesh, (General, first bench) read what you have written".*

*Ramesh read whatever he had written and was told by teacher to sit down.*

*Teacher - "Pramil (ST, third bench), you read.*

*Boy - Yah ek ped hai.*

*Teacher - Ye kahani aise shuru hota hai? Baitho. Sunil.*

*Boy - Ek ped me bahut sa phal hai.*

*Teacher - Achcha, dikhai pad raha hai kya (smiled)? You read (pointing to the ST boy on the last bench)".*

*Boy – (not clear in reading)*

*The student was stopped by the teacher for not reading clearly.*

*Teacher - "Kya, kya bolta hai, samajh nahi aata. Mantar (chant) jaise bolta hai. Baitho".*

After the boys' turn, girls were asked to read the story. Two-three girls from first bench were heard by the teacher. And then,

*Teacher- "Sunita (ST, second bench), read.*

*Girl - Ek aadmi tha. Wah topi bechta tha. Ek din aadmi dusra gaon topi bechne ja raha tha. Garmi ka din tha. Rasta me use ek ped mila. Wah apna topi rakh kar ped ke niche so gaya. Ped par bandar rahta tha. Bandar topi uthakar ped par chadh gaya. Aadmi achanak utha to dekha, ki uska topi us jagah par nahi tha. Aadmi idhar udhar dekhne laga, phir ped par dekha to bandar topi pahne baitha tha. Aadmi sochne laga ki mera topi kaise wapas aayega?*

*Teacher - Very good!*

*Teacher- You read (to second bench girl, ST).*

*Girl - Nahi likhe hain sir.*

*Teacher - Kuch to bolo.*

*Girl - Ek ped tha. Ped par chiria rahti thi...*

*Teacher - Chiria bandar ban gaya aur bandar aadmi ban gaya. Baitho. You all have written different stories and you are so many in numbers that it's impossible to hear everyone's stories. Now I will make a story".*

The teacher narrated a story, a well known one that I had read when I was in school. As the interaction with students suggested, the teacher only appreciated one or two students for narrating the story similar to his. Some students were not permitted to read further for wrong beginning. Students were not appreciated for not being fluent in speaking or reading. The teacher ignored the language problem that students face due to language differences with that of teacher. Instead, they were smiled at, mocked and criticised by the teacher for not writing properly. They were not provided a scaffold or guided or encouraged to construct their own story out of these words but were subtly disempowered by the teacher to develop their ability of thinking. They were not provided any space for their own imagination, creativity and initiative to explore. These were weakened by the teacher's limited knowledge of the text-books, not allowing them to think beyond that boundary. The message conveyed by teachers was that their knowledge (limited to the text-books) was superior to that of their students. The result was that disinterest, boredom and disengagement from classroom transaction easily followed.

*Language, Codes and Norms:* Despite several policy recommendations and constitutional provision (article 350 A) of mother tongue for linguistic minorities at primary level, in practice there is no education in tribal languages (Nambissan 2000). It was true with the school that was studied where language imperialism continued and the initial instruction in mother tongue (kurukh) in first two years of primary level was missing due to unavailability of text books in mother tongue.

As some researchers have pointed out, non-tribal teachers tend to see the home languages of tribal children as barriers to education. This was reflected in teachers' perceptions about tribal languages. The non-tribal (SC) teacher of class VI said,

> "The languages of 'adivasis' are a big barrier. So many times I ask children to try to speak in Hindi with their family and friends. They don't speak in Hindi. Especially these tribal children speak in 'kurukh', and that's why their pronunciations don't improve. For example, if you ask them to say 'dhoti', they will say 'dhuti' or if you ask them to say 'dekchi', they will say 'dikchi'. These are some of the words that they can't say properly. Even our tribal teachers also have language problem. If you ask them to say 'teyis' (23), they will say 'tayis'. This also affects children's learning". (Teachers' interview)

The teacher instead of appreciating and encouraging tribal students to express themselves in their own language compelled them to speak Hindi fluently with right pronunciation, not only in the class but also at home with their family and friends. Their own languages were denigrated causing them feel discomfort.

Learning in Hindi and English, which are languages of the dominant cultural group was made compulsory and teachers ridiculed rural/tribal children for wrong linguistic expressions (pronunciations) and also for not learning the codes and norms of the schools. The English language teacher felt that the primary lessons that children need to be taught are proper ways of speaking and representing one self. The teacher wanted tribal students (who felt shy to respond or interact) to learn to speak fluent English but his emphasis on codes of presentation and linguistic expression (pronunciation) taking specific children and their ways of speaking as examples had the negative effect of further "silencing" them. For instance, during an English lesson the teacher tried to teach 'Hinglish' (a fusion of Hindi and English language) and also to present oneself smartly and boldly. The teacher tried to teach a third language to students who had difficulty even to speak the second language (Hindi), the official medium of instruction. Thus, we see that language differences between home and school creates barriers for children to learn smoothly and teacher's insensitivity adds to the children's woes.

*Labelling and Categorising:* Labelling is a social construction and is a sign of control and domination. It is used to place value on students' actions. Labelling enables teachers and others to "differentiate students according to their 'ability' and their possession of particular kinds of cultural capital" (Apple, 2004:123). Tribal children were categorised, stratified and discriminated as socially and culturally inferior by the teachers and peers. Students of first/second rows were seen as 'good students' by the teachers and the rest (tribal students sitting at the back) were identified as poor in studies and were labelled as **'lofar'**. When asked about the back benchers, the Hindi teacher (General) said:

> "They (tribal students) are **'lofar'**. They don't bother about studies. They just come to school. They don't care what happen in class. They never pay attention. Now the rule is that you are not supposed to fail any student in the class. These students (tribal students) have become worst because of this rule. Their studies have also become poor. They don't work hard. They don't study at all".

Teachers had negative impression and categorised the back benchers (tribal students) as "dull", inattentive and "slow learners" for not grasping and responding in the class and were labelled as 'Jharkhandi Sarkar' (*'kole'/ 'adivasi'*) for not completing the class work on time. It shows teacher's prejudice about tribes whom they see as intellectually backward.

*Bunking and Being Away:* Two types of students' absence were seen in the classrooms, i.e. mental as well as physical. 'Mental' absence is being present physically but not mentally in the class while teaching. It is also called day-dreaming which Goffman (1968) termed "'being away', a kind of mental removal from the scene" (as cited in Talib 1992:86). Students especially back benchers (tribal children) were found day-dreaming during classroom transaction which according to Talib (1992) is a sign of isolation of students from the rest of the class who are given more attention by the teachers.

Many times they were seen in removal activities such as making paper toys (box) and playing with it, playing with the pen, yawning, peeping outside the window instead of doing class work or listening to the teacher, and dreaming while the teacher explained or asked questions. This was due to teacher's differential attitude and behaviour with these students. Teachers made no effort to know what was happening at the back of the class and tended to leave back benchers on their own, thinking that they would not improve at all. In response to this attitude of teachers, tribal children rejected to follow the classroom activities by indulging to remain silent while the teacher asked questions or by following their own will without bothering about teacher's anger or scolding. Not only mental, but physical absence from the class or school was also evident to save themselves from boredom and scolding for not completing the homework. For instance, class VIII children were seen bunking Sanskrit period for not memorising *"shabd-roop"* and *"dhatu-roop"*. They rejected teacher's authority as they were aware of her regime and the way of teaching. Some tribal students believed that instead of wasting their time at school it is better to work at home/field, graze cattle or take care of their siblings. Such behaviour of these tribal students shows that they developed their own spaces to move away from the monotonous pedagogy of the classroom and school.

## Perceptions about Self

Pupils participate in formal and informal activities inside the school and try to see themselves from other's point of view and weigh whether they fulfil the criteria to reach that goal or not. Each individual interacts according to group identification, attitudes and beliefs. This helps them understand and recognise them 'selves' and eventually develop perception about their 'self'.

It was observed that both teachers and peers influenced in the construction of 'self'. Tribal children hesitated to communicate with their teachers and non-tribal counterparts because they felt that they were not competent as their peers and, thereby reinforced their own sense of 'inferiority'. Negative impressions of teachers and peers had a detrimental impact on tribal students' perceptions making them develop poor self-confidence and discouraging them to reach the goals set by the teachers (others).

However, awareness regarding academic situation was also evident in them. Comparing themselves with other castes students they viewed themselves as poor in studies because they could not 'grasp easily', did not take tuitions, and were unable to answer in the class and also in exams. Impoverished home environment did not provide money, time, facilities, support, guidance or motivation for their studies and this led tribal students to remain quiet, secluded, passive, non-participative and uninvolved in school. Also, they did not receive any support from school for the development of a positive sense of self. Thus, identity of self is constructed based on different treatment, motivation and environment.

## Conclusion

The above study of the ground realities of schooling of tribal children derives the conclusion that tribal children were included in mass enrollment; still it had been a discriminatory inclusion. Little change was evident in the educational status of tribal children as seen in the study. They continued to be excluded through discriminatory classroom processes that seemed to have kept alive the traditional dominant culture of mainstream society. The school and classrooms persisted to be alien spaces for tribal children – for the school curriculum did not take into account or utilize their natural and social environment, culture, language, everyday experiences and resources that were brought by children.

The issue that emerges from the study is that tribal children continued to be 'back benchers' and lacked access to teacher's attention due to teacher's preferences for 'good' students and lack of rotation in seating arrangement. Discrimination existed not only at the level of curriculum, but also at the behaviour and preconceived notions and attitudes of teachers that were equally responsible for existing disparities. Most tribal students therefore were victims to these biases, prejudices and negative attitudes. Teachers were seen not interacting with tribal students and had negative stereotypes - saw them as 'weak' and 'dull' students. Classroom transaction was based on conventional pedagogy of teaching, i.e. limited to text-books and rote memorisation. No teaching aids, no activities or space were provided for student's imagination, creativity and initiative to explore. Teachers' negative perceptions about tribal languages provided them as reasons to teach tribal children the language, and codes and norms of the dominant group to civilize them to survive in the modern world. They were differentiated and categorised according to their 'ability'. Conventional pedagogy and neglect by the teachers compelled these students to 'being away' from the class mentally as well as physically. All these factors thereby influenced the development of self confidence, character, and personality and facilitate learning abilities of tribal children that led to their poor performance and unsatisfactory educational growth.

Thus, there is the need to address the critical role that culture plays in the education of tribal children. Incorporation of diverse and inclusive pedagogies and practices are essential to encourage participation and to enhance tribal children's learning. Mother tongue, in the early stages at primary level is critical to build child's potential and self confidence. Teachers need to be sensitized in the teacher education programme about the marginalised groups, their culture and languages and home school linkages in order to tackle problems related to a tribal child's education.

## REFERENCES

Apple, M.W. (2004). 'Cultural Politics and the Text' in Stephan J. Ball (ed.), *Reader in Sociology of Education*. London: Routledge Falmer.

Bhattacharjee, N. (1999). 'Through the Looking Glass: Gender Socialization in a Primary School' in T.S. Saraswathi (ed.), *Culture, Socialization and Human Development: Theory Research and Applications in India*. New Delhi: Sage.

Brint, S. (1998). *Schools and Societies*. London: Pine Forge Press.

Cohen, L. and Laurence Manion. (1983). Multicultural Classroom. London: Croom Helm.

Delpit, L.D. (1997). 'The Silence Dialogue: Power and Pedagogy in Educating Other People's Children' in Halsey, Lauder, Brown and Wells (ed.), *Education: Culture, Economy and Society*. New York: OUP.

Freire, P. (1970). *Pedagogy of the Oppressed*. London: Penguin.

GOI (2001 a). Office of the Registrar General of India Report.

Government of India. (2007 a). *Selected Educational Statistics*, 2004-05, Department of Higher Education, MHRD. New Delhi.

Lakra, Abhineet Kala. (2008). *Ethnicity and Classroom Processes: An Exploratory Study of a School in Jharkhand*. Unpublished M.Phil. Dissertation, JNU.

Nambissan G. B. (2000). 'Identity, Exclusion and the Education of Tribal Communities' in Rekha Wazir (ed.), *The Gender Gap in Basic Education: NGOs as Change Agents*. New Delhi: Sage.

Shaw, B. (1981). Educational Practice and sociology: an Introduction. Oxford: martin & Robertson.

Subrahmaniyan, R. (2005). 'Education Exclusion and the Developmental State' in Radhika Chopra and Patricia Jeffery (ed.), *Educational regimes in Contemporary India*. New Delhi: Sage.

Sujatha, K. (1996). Single teacher Schools in tribal Areas: A Study of Girijan Vidya Vikas kendras in Andhra Pradesh. New Delhi: NUEPA.

Talib, Mohammad. (1992). 'Ideology, Curriculum and class construction: Observations from a School in a Working Class settlement in Delhi', *Sociological Bulletin*, vol.41 (1&2):81-95.

Woods, P. (1983). *Sociology and the School: An Interactionist Viewpoint*. London: Routledge & Kegan Paul.

# 4

# Inclusive Education of Children with Special Needs in Schools of Delhi

## *A Critique*

***Sailaja Chennat***

We, in the developing world are still groping in the dark trying to answer the 'what' and 'how' questions of education of Children with Special Need (CSN). This may account for the inadequate and unplanned provisions that have been made by the various governments. The provision for CSN across developing countries has often been regarded as a privilege rather than a right (Alur, 2001). Most developing countries, if not all, are progressive in terms of formulation of national policies for the education of CSN. Some of the policies have such recommendation as to give concrete meaning to the idea of equalizing educational opportunities for all children irrespective of their physical and mental conditions (Alur, 2001). Like the National Policy of India, other countries like Botswana, Nigeria etc have included in the policies that such children should be educated alongside their normal counterparts in the ordinary schools. Despite these, the dreams of most people with disabilities are yet to be realized, in areas of adequate educational provisions, employment, and support services (Abosi & Koay, 2008).

'Inclusion' is the catch word of this century used in the field of education. It relates to people and community that value and respect diversity among people and diligent about overcoming barriers. But what exactly does inclusion mean? Is it perceived differently by different people? Does inclusion really work across nations? This still remains to be answered. It all started with 'special educational needs'. In the last century, concern about children with special needs led to 'special schools' providing 'special education'. It is difficult to find convincing evidence that pupils do better in special schools. (Topping and Maloney, 2005). The end of the century saw the paradigm shift to 'integration' or 'reintegration' of pupils with special needs into 'mainstream' schools. Much of this movement geared to political and public opinion towards integration stemmed more from ethical arguments rather than functional rationale. Even before 'integration' became widespread in practice, the rhetoric moved on and 'inclusion' became the new buzzword. The concept of educational inclusion is now seen in the wider perspective of social inclusion, implying concern for all those, of all ages marginalized on the basis of language, class, religion, gender, region, origin or capabilities. These concerns are debated in the context of equal opportunities. 'Equal opportunities' does not mean simply treating everyone equally, as this would only help to perpetuate the existing inequalities rather, it implies treating different people with differentiation so as to ensure that they all have equal opportunities to maximize their potential. In this research study, the perspective of inclusive education is delimited to that of children with special needs only.

## Understanding of Inclusion

The present status of 'inclusion' is, as an international descriptor of a particular interface of both ethos and practice, a philosophy and practice or a value and practice. A child could be in a regular class and yet be feeling excluded because of the attitude of peer group and teachers. Inclusion has an emotional content and involves the whole school as a community with positive and compassionate attitude to children with disabilities and their right to enjoy studying in the regular school (adapted from Topping and Maloney, 2005).

*Indicators of an inclusive school*

The attitude and philosophy of inclusion is reflected in the whole school as a community and the membership to the school is open, positive and diverse; not selective or rejecting.

The school is barrier free, accessible to all its members, physically in terms of the building and play ground, educationally in terms of curricula, support systems and methods of transaction.

The school promotes collaboration: it works with, rather than competitively against, other schools.

The school promotes equality; it provides a forum where all members have rights and responsibilities, with the same opportunity to benefit from and take part in the education process.

## National Status of Children with Special Needs (CSN)

India has approximately 40 to 80 million persons with disability (PWD). But low literacy, few jobs and widespread social stigma are making disabled people among the most excluded in India. Illiteracy rates are very high for all PWD, but extreme for those with severe disabilities. Around 38 per cent of CSN aged 6-13 are out of school, with the rates much higher for certain disabilities. Almost three quarters of those with severe disabilities are illiterate, and the same share do not attend school and even for those with mild disabilities, the illiteracy rate is around half. While policies are important, it is educational outcomes that matter. It is very clear that both educational attainment of all PWD and current attendance of CSN are very poor and far below national averages.

It is a significant point to note that India has gradually increased the focus on children and adults with special needs, and that inclusive education in regular schools has become a primary policy objective (World Bank Report, 2007).

## The International Scenario

The international scenario is not very encouraging either. 33-40 per cent of out of school children worldwide have disabilities (UNESCO, 2004). For the severely disabled, just over 10 per cent have achieved middle school or higher education, while even for moderately disabled people the share is only 20 per cent. Close to one third of children with only mild disabilities are not in school. These are children who need no aids/ appliances to participate, and should in principle not be significantly more difficult than other children to bring into the school system.

## Research Study — Delhi's Schools

The study was carried out in the schools of Delhi to critically examine the system of inclusive education in a selected sample of state run schools of Delhi.

*Objectives of the study*: The objectives of the study were to develop an understanding of the processes and issues related to inclusive education in the state run schools from the perspective of Heads, teachers and students with an in depth case study of one school and to study the perceptions about and attitude towards the philosophy of inclusion, of teachers and Heads.

*Population and sample of the study*: From the population of around 4880 state run schools of Delhi, a sample of 20 schools from 5 each from the regions of the state, viz: North, East, West, South and Central were selected randomly for the study

*Nature and source of data*: Data collected was all descriptive and the sources were the Head, teachers, students, documents of the schools, classroom processes and the school activities in total.

*Instruments of data collection*: All the tools used for data collection were developed by the researcher. They were modified and improved after an initial data collection to ensure their validity and reliability. An *observation schedule* was used to study the classroom processes and school activities outside the classrooms and *semi-structured interview* schedule and *open ended questionnaire* were used for collecting data from students, teachers and Head.

*Analysis:* Content analysis of the responses and observations was carried out to form categories, corresponding to the objectives of the study.

## FINDINGS OF THE STUDY

Data collected from teachers, Head and from observations have been presented to give the status of inclusive education in the selected schools. All the 20 schools selected for the study had CSN and had an *Integrated Education for the Disabled Children (IEDC) Cell,* a state sponsored scheme for the education of CSN, with a Coordinator, with all details like name and other personal data of each CSN, type of disability, whether certificate of disability was submitted, and if yes, percentage of disability etc.

### Data From Teachers

80 per cent teachers said that they did not know the details of CSN, and that there was IEDC cell which had all details. Apart from this, they did not know about the functions of the IEDC cell. 20 per cent of teachers had some knowledge about the type and the percentage of disability of CSN in their class. 80 per cent of teachers did not know about the category of challenge unless it was a visible challenge like the visually challenged, hearing challenged with a hearing aid or an orthopaedically challenged. Among the teachers interviewed for the study only 4 understood the word 'challenged'. They were all familiar with the word 'handicapped' and 80 per cent were aware of the word 'disabled'. 85 per cent of the teachers were not aware of the national educational policy for CSN. Apart from the identified CSN, according to 40 per cent of teachers there were many 'handicapped children' in their classes. To the question of how they could be sure that these children were handicapped, the answer was, 'from their behaviour' in the class.

All teachers were of the opinion that all CSN should get financial help, aids, reservation in job etc. 80 per cent were not aware of what it means to be a CSN. According to them, only physically handicapped children came under the category of CSN. To the question of whether they could relate any incident which had impacted them as a teacher of CSN, 70 per cent of them said there was nothing that they could think of. 30 per cent of teachers narrated incidents of quarrel and redressal in the class among CSN and the other students.

*Children with Special Needs (CSN)*

50 per cent of teachers said they could not give any special attention to CSN in their class. 50 per cent of the teachers did take note of the needs of CSN and brought in some changes like, seating a hearing challenged child or a partially sighted child in the front bench, or making an academically bright child sit beside a CSN for peer support and motivation. But for these teachers, CSN meant visually, hearing or orthopaedically challenged students only, which are the very apparent, visible hard disabilities.

And 60 per cent of the teachers had not identified any student in the class with special need apart from those already admitted as per records with the IEDC Coordinator.

*Attitude Towards Inclusion of CSN*

The 75 per cent of teachers were in favour of inclusion, provided adequate matching facilities were provided to CSN. 25 per cent were of the opinion that this is not the right policy and that it was more justified to have special schools for CSN.

*Assessment Camp* (Camps organized by the state for assessment of CSN who were not assessed before their admission to schools)

The 80 per cent of teachers did not have a clear understanding of what the assessment camps were, what their functions were, nor did they think that it was necessary for them to know about all these matters. They said that the IEDC coordinator was entrusted with all these 'data' of inclusive education of CSN. 20 per cent had some idea that such camps were held and that students were sent there, although they did not know further about how the assessment informed the decisions taken regarding teaching learning in the class.

*Parental Support*

In 75 per cent of the schools regular parent-teacher meetings (PTM) were not organised. This problem escalated in rural areas where most of the parents were just not available as they worked as labourers on daily wage basis. They were uneducated and had no clue regarding any of the special needs of their child. In two schools teachers were so frustrated by this ignorance of the parents that they did not want any support from parents. They had helped themselves settle with the idea that such parents have irreversible mindset and that nothing could be done to urge them to provide any support to their child or to the teachers. In 25 per cent of schools, PTM were organized occasionally, but the participation from the parents was not encouraging. All of the teachers were of the view was that unless parents worked in tandem with the teachers, CSN could not learn well with the regular peer group. 85 per cent of the teachers were of the view that parents of CSN should also be given counselling, for which time management was a major issue which had to be tackled at the administrative level. Some of them also pointed out the regularly organized monthly PTM s in private schools as an important factor leading to better care and nurture of CSN, as compared to the plight in these state run schools. In such PTM s some counselling of the parents always happened by which CSN and parents were both helped and reassured. It was also added that these PTM s were possible because of lower strength of the classes in these schools, generally below 50.

*Peer Group*

It was observed that almost all CSN had friends. Generally normal teasing of CSN was a common problem, but this was offset with the fact they were helped well by the peer group whenever the need arose. In 20 per cent of the schools, the teachers said that some times CSN created disturbances in the class which actually hampered the curricular transactions. Among these, in 15 per cent of the schools, most of the teachers regularly counselled the regular students to be cooperative and supportive to CSN.

*Sharing with Colleagues*

Around 40 per cent of the teachers did not discuss any problems or special incidents related to CSN with their colleagues. The reason stated was general lack of time and pressure to complete much other important works within the available school time. 50 per cent of them discussed occasionally but not so often. One important thing that came out was that those teachers who discussed CSN with their colleagues were able to deal more effectively with a CSN with insights from the colleague who also taught the same child. They shared their experiences of addressing the problems faced in the classroom and discussed the academic growth of this CSN so that they could chalk out common strategies of teaching and assessment for that particular child with special need (CSN).

*Awareness about IEDC*

Almost 80 per cent of the teachers were not aware of the guidelines given by IEDC cell or about the role of an IEDC coordinator, or how CSN could be benefited by the IEDC cell. All the teachers said that IEDC coordinators from the Office of Education visited once in a while to take the statistics of these children and to provide the funds, and other assistance set apart for CSN. According to them IEDC Cell meant centre for mainly record keeping.

The cell has the following data:

- Class wise particulars of CSN, like name and personal data, type of disability, percentage of disability; whether aid/

appliance has been received under the IEDC. There is a compilation of the above mentioned data of each class.

- Guidelines given to the teachers and Head regarding the symptoms of different categories of challenge like, autism, cerebral palsy, attention deficit hyperactive disorder, visually challenge, so as to help with identification of such challenges among children .
- Assessment camp-expenditure norms for each camp, assessment certificate of each student.
- Questionnaire for students—with questions covering most of the details like the onset of the challenge, type of challenge, reason for the challenge, whether anyone else in the family has the same challenge, distance from home to school, , whether medical treatment has been received etc. These questionnaires are generally filled up by the Coordinator with help from the parents.
- Data of all CSN in the school for each year.
- Record of financial assistance given to CSN.

**Facilities**

It was observed that 95 per cent of the schools had ramps and special toilet for orthopedically challenged. They were aware about the provision of extra time and a scribe in the state level exams organized for the X Class and the XII Class students. But according to their understanding there were no special arrangements made in the school during term end exams.

Teachers from 3 schools said that doctors and counsellors used to visit the school to give their services for CSN once or twice in a year. 70 per cent teachers complained about non availability of suitable learning aids for the CSN, especially the hearing challenged and the visually challenged learners.

**Classroom Transaction**

It was also found that 90 per cent of teachers were "patient" while dealing with CSN. Teachers said that CSN needed empathy, support, positive reinforcement, special attention and more secure environment. But of these 40 per cent were not able to differentiate between empathy and sympathy. 60 per cent of teachers said that they were able to address the needs of CSN. To the question of how they were able to address the needs, their response was not forthcoming or was not to the point. Some of them said that 'they needed special attention and motivation'. 95 per cent of the teachers did not have knowledge of curricular adaptations or improvised assessment procedures. They did not have any individualized teaching plan. 75 per cent of the teachers stated that many of the students had concentration problem and that it was a major task to get them to listen to what was happening in the classroom transactions. 90 per cent of these teachers also stated that many of the students were very slow in noting down whatever was written on the blackboard, were slow in answering any question posed to them. These problems, according to the teachers dampened the momentum of the transactions in the classroom and they added that it was difficult to tackle these issues. No teacher had made any improvisation in the content or mode of transaction in order to help the CSN. They also gave the same homework to CSN as given to other students. Time constraint was cited as the reason for this situation too.

*Counselling*

Similarly the results show that 40 per cent of teachers never counselled CSN ever. 20 per cent of them did regular counselling; remaining 40 per cent also did counselling but once in a while. According to one teacher, counselling helped to boost up the morale of the SNC slowly and significantly. 85 per cent of teachers did not consult parents of CSN at all, leave alone counselling them, as parents did not come to school regularly. One teacher said that teachers met parents only at the time of admission and never later. It was stated by all the teachers who said that they counselled the CSN that they felt helpless while counselling as they themselves did not have proper understanding about the nature and needs of the CSN. All of them opined that regular counselling of CSN would definitely bear fruitful results like, increased participation in CCA, more self confidence, better regularity etc.

*Support from Head*

To the question whether they got any motivation from their Head, 70 per cent replied in affirmative, but none of them was able to describe how he/she got motivation. Remaining 30 per cent said they didn't get any motivation from their Head regarding CSN at all. 50 per cent of them generally didn't get any suggestion from their Head regarding CSN. In fact two teachers said that last year (2008-09), the Principal had refused to give admission to a challenged child.

**Training Programmes for Teachers**

Only 80 per cent of teachers had attended at least one seminar regarding CSN and apart from seminars workshops with some practical inputs were not organized. As a result, they had a lack of understanding regarding CSN. 60 per cent of them did not take these seminars seriously and said that they attended these seminars as they were mandatory and not because they thought that inputs from such seminars would help them with the issues in the classrooms.

*Problem Areas Identified*

*Perspective on Inclusion:* Most of the teachers and the Head did not apparently believe in inclusive education as a philosophy or a value. But they saw it as a Governmental policy which could not, but, be adhered to.

*High Strength of Students:* One of the major points that came up was high student-teacher ratio. 60 per cent of the schools had more than 70 students in a class. They were already stressed out with the large number of students in the classes, as a result of which, they were not able to give optimum time to even the regular students.

The areas where all the teachers felt helpless were insufficient attendance, improper financial help and insufficient awareness of parents'. One teacher said that the area where he felt helpless was 'social acceptability', which according to him was acceptance by himself and the students.

*Time Constraint:* This was the major problem stated by all the teachers. They had six periods of teaching per day on an average and had to complete other paper work in the remaining time like implementation of welfare schemes viz; money distribution for uniform, stationery, textbooks etc, financial assistance to children of Scheduled Cast and Scheduled Tribe categories, assistance in the mid day meal distribution etc, all on a regular basis, apart from the seasonal duties of polling. It was stated by many teachers that they did more clerical work than teaching work.

*Teacher Support:* All the teachers expressed the lack of know how about the nature and needs of CSN and the total absence of proper training provided to address the needs of these learners in the pre-service course they had all undergone. 85 per cent of the teachers said that the components of Inclusive Education in the programme of in-service training courses organized by the government were inadequate to equip the teachers as effective practitioners. Moreover they stated that these inputs were very conceptual and not field related practical inputs. 85 per cent teachers said that they had no onsite support for many specialists to address the challenges they faced.

*Poor Attendance:* All the teachers said that the attendance of the children in general and of CSN in particular was a major issue that they had to tackle. Cases of children working temporarily as milk, flower and vegetable vendors, especially when they had to substitute their ill father or mother were common in the schools which affected the attendance of even regular children.

*Follow up of CSN:* No school had any data regarding CSN who had dropped out or passed out.

*Suggestions from Teachers*

*Curriculum*: Total 50 per cent of teachers did not give any suggestion regarding improvisations necessary in the syllabus vis-a vis each category of challenge. One suggestion given by 30 per cent of the teachers was that the syllabus should be more practical and close to their daily life. For facilitating effective learning, special books with larger and colourful fonts etc as learning aids were suggested. All of them were in favour of regular Co Curricular Activities for CSN.

*Assessment*: It is almost 70 per cent of them did not give any suggestions regarding assessment procedures at all. 30 per cent of them suggested more oral tests than written tests. One of the teachers suggested continuous and comprehensive evaluation system for assessment. 80 per cent of teachers said that question papers should be same for CSN as for regular students. Two suggested that question papers should be more objective and simple.

*Infrastructural facilities*: Regarding infrastructural facilities teachers suggested that ramp with railings, wide door, special toilet, proper guide map, additional space for personal care, additional mechanical aids etc should be provided to CSN.

*Parental support*: All teachers opined that parental support was indispensable for the development of CSN. They even suggested that for ensuring this, parents should be given incentives to come to the meetings organized for them, by way of financial assistance.

*Teacher support*: Onsite support for teachers was a strong point suggested by all the teachers. All the teachers recommended that there should be at least one special educator in each school to help and provide onsite support to the teachers to identify, understand and help the CSN in the classes. Additionally, regular in service workshops for teachers should be organized with inputs on the nature and needs of the CSN, development and implementation of Individual Lesson Plans with corresponding assessment methods and also ways and means of counselling the CSN. One teacher said that workshops for teachers should be more practical giving them field related suggestions rather than being theoretical as they generally were. It was also suggested that CSN doing well could participate in the workshops so as to motivate the teachers to work hard towards successful inclusive practices. There was a strong suggestion from 85 per cent of the teachers that financial help to CSN must be increased to bring these children to schools. One teacher even suggested for a trained attendant for CSN in each class.

Almost 95 per cent clearly said that all pre-service Teacher Education programmes should have a compulsory course in the education of CSN.

## Data from IEDC Coordinator

All IEDC Coordinators, one from each school had all records in place regarding CSN of their own school. They did not have any special orientation for discharging their duties, nor did they have any monitory benefits. Also, it was said that this was all in addition to their regular work load of teaching which made it very taxing for them to maintain all records. According to them, these records were all kept with them and were not referred to by the Head or teachers. They got regular e mail communication from the IEDC CELL, Directorate of Education regarding tasks related to CSN and their activities were regularly monitored by the visits of a representative from this cell. In these visits, records were checked, the distribution of financial assistance, supply of appliances, assessment processes etc were all streamlined.

## Data from Heads

### *Admission Policy*

It was found that 80 per cent of the Heads stated that they were open to admitting any type of CSN as that was the guideline given to them and that they generally got visually challenged, who were partially sighted, partially hearing or orthopedically challenged who could move, but slowly. 20 per cent of the Heads said that they got severely challenged students for admission in the past 3 or 4 years who were guided to take admission in special schools. To the question of why they did so, the answer was that their teachers had no training to address the needs of CSN except for some inputs received in in-service training programmes, which according to them were in sufficient.

### *Attitude towards inclusion of CSN*

90 per cent of had positive attitude to inclusion of CSN, but said only mildly challenged could be accommodated in the present situation. 10 per cent were of the opinion that CSN should be given special education. One of the main points put forth to support this argument was that the large numbers of students in regular schools deprived CSN of any personal attention which they need all through.

### *IEDC Cell/CSN*

All the Heads stated that the IEDC Cell was functional in their schools and that all information regarding CSN was maintained by the Coordinator of this Cell. When asked about the details of the CSN they had in the school 80 per cent of the Heads did not have any clear idea, but said that data could be taken from IEDC CELL. 20 per cent of the Heads talked about some details of a few CSN students.

*Assessment Camps*

All the Heads said about the assessment camps and the way students were assessed by experts like doctors and psychologist, audiologist, ophthalmologist etc. They knew that CSN who did not have an assessment done earlier benefited from these camps.

*Assessment Records*

70 per cent of the Heads asked for assessment certificate of CSN at the time of admission. All Heads said that they had no time for reading and understanding these documents and that the IEDC Coordinator was supposed to look into all these matters. 20 per cent said that not all students had such assessment records, although they tried to procure these later, they could not succeed in most of the cases. All the Heads said that no review of the disability was done once the CSN was admitted. All the Heads understood that the assessment records were solely for admission purpose and for procuring assistance from the Government, and hence these records were in the safe custody of the IEDC Coordinator.

*Parental Support*

Almost 70 per cent of Heads said that parent teacher meetings (PTMs) were not organized although there were attempts earlier to organize these meetings which were given up as parents did not cooperate. 30 per cent of the Heads said PTMs were organized occasionally, although the participation from parents was not encouraging. This apathy of the parents, they pointed as a major reason for the lack of improvement among most of the cases of CSN.

*Support to Teachers*

60 per cent of the Heads said that whenever teachers came to them for any support they redressed the issues in the way they thought best and that IEDC Cell Coordinator was also taken into this loop for support mechanism. All these Heads sated that the problems were related to the behaviour problems of CSN and how this hampered with discipline of the class and never learning or assessment related issues. 40 per cent of Heads said that their teachers did not approach them with issues related to CSN.

*Training Programmes for Heads*

All of the Heads said that they had attended seminars conducted by the state for sensitizing the Heads towards the needs of the CSN. 50 per cent opined that these were not sufficient for the effective discharge of their duties as Head.

*Training Programmes for Teachers*

All of the Heads said that their teachers regularly attended the in service training programmes organized b the state. 90 per cent of the Heads did not have any comment on the content of these programmes as they did not know the content. All of them knew that these programmes had a session on CSN and inclusive education.

*Meeting and Discussion with Teachers*

70 per cent of Heads had no regular meetings with teachers to discuss the issues related to CSN. 30 per cent of Heads discussed with teachers individually regarding CSN, although there were no formal meetings, and that generally, issues related to discipline came up in such discussions or regarding supply of some aids like hearing aid, specks etc.

**Observations in the Classroom**

Two Classrooms each from 10 (out of 20 selected) schools with CSN were observed making it 20 observations in total. Most of the classes observed had more than 60 students. The CSN included partially sighted, hearing challenged, including 'totally deaf' as per the teachers, some mentally challenged and orthopedically challenged. Teachers were seen to be generally conscious about the CSN, to the extent that they were seated in the front row, especially the partially sighted and the hearing challenged. The orthopedically challenged were allowed to sit while interacting in the class although the general norm of schools was that all students should stand up while interacting. In 45 per cent of the classes, teachers were seen to go to the students individually and check their writing and reading. Apart from these, no other special improvisations in the content, transactions or assessment techniques were observed. Use of visual aids was conspicuously lacking which would support the learning of all children except the blind.

*Observations in the Playground and in General*

It was seen that almost all CSN had friends although a few were seen to be isolated. Most of these children were orthopedically or hearing challenged. When asked why they didn't have friends, they said they preferred it that way and that they didn't feel bad about it. It was seen that there was ramp and special toilets for the orthopaedically challenged learners in all schools. But as there were no learners on wheel chair, both these facilities were not used in 60 per cent of the schools.

**IEDC CELL**

The cell has the following data:

- Class-wise particulars of CSN, like name and personal data, type of disability, percentage of disability; whether aid/

appliance has been received under the IEDC. There is a compilation of the above mentioned data of each class.

- Guidelines given to the teachers and Head regarding the symptoms of different categories of challenge like, autism, cerebral palsy, attention deficit hyperactive disorder, visually challenge, so as to help with identification of such challenges among children.
- Assessment camp-expenditure norms for each camp, assessment certificate of each student
- Questionnaire for students- with questions covering most of the details like the onset of the challenge, type of challenge, reason for the challenge, whether anyone else in the family has the same challenge, distance from home to school, whether medical treatment has been received etc. These questionnaires are generally filled up by the Coordinator with help from the parents.
- Data of all CSN in the school for each year for the present year and previous 3 years)
- Record of financial assistance given to CSN in the year 2005-06 wheel chair which are not used as there are no CSN on wheel chair.

**Inferences from Interpretive Discussion**

*School System*

The system is awakening, though slowly, and is responding to the cause of CSN by providing infrastructural facilities, financial assistance and by attempting to improve the quality of teaching learning. There is definitely enough evidence collected from all schools to prove that the attitude of Heads and teachers towards CSN is moving towards the positive side.

*The General Attitude Towards and Awareness about CSN*

The general awareness among teachers regarding the nature and needs of the SNC seems to be inadequate to tackle the issues in the classrooms. The limited understanding of CSN as physically challenged among most of the teachers seems to be linked to many of the problems arising in the schools. This does not in any way get resolved by support from the Head. Most of the Heads are equally ignorant about the academic and emotional needs of CSN and the corresponding curricular adaptations required for facilitating their learning.

*Classroom Processes*

There is a general lack of insights among teachers and Heads about ways and means of identifying CSN from their behaviour in the classrooms and learning outcomes and a lack of empathy and sensitivity to address the corresponding emotional and academic needs. Teachers are not adequately trained in designing a content-pedagogy package customized as per the needs of CSN. These realities reflect on the inadequate efforts put forth in designing in service training programmes and onsite support programmes for the teachers by the system.

Case study reveals that there are partially sighted and hearing challenged students who are not in the IEDC records. This reflects on the fact that the system is not efficient in identifying those who are not so 'visibly' challenged. There could be many others who are not able to cope up with the regular learners, are ignored and are forced to drop out in due course.

*Parental Support*

Teachers and Heads meet the parents only during admissions and this is seen as a major issue by the teachers and the Head of all the schools. Parental support is seen by all teachers and Heads as crucial for the learning and personality development of any CSN. With groups of parents who don't show up even when called for Parent Teacher Meetings (PTM s) organized by some of the schools, problems of education of CSN get compounded. In fact the apathy of the parents has de-motivated the other schools from organizing PTMs where these meetings were attempted earlier.

*Peer Support*

The finding that all CSN had friends and that they were very supportive of the CSN points to the possibilities of developing better collaborative learning and peer tutorial systems to help the CSN.

*Sharing of Classroom Experiences*

Lack of sharing with colleagues regarding the nature and needs of CSN, curricular adaptations or assessment methods, is seen as a major lacuna in the school system. All CSN of a class are generally engaged in learning by a group of at least 3 to 4 teachers in all secondary and senior secondary classes. Sharing of experiences of these teachers would enhance the quality of teaching learning. In fact the insights developed through classroom experiences could be much more enriching to the teachers as practitioners. Sharing of practice and debriefing the transactional procedures are great ways of developing small theories of one's own which may augment or complement the official knowledge gained from pre or in service programmes which are anyway inadequate. For this to be achieved, co analysis of practice by teachers has to be a routine activity of teachers.

Facilitating attitudinal change and a paradigm shift to a reflective path in professional development seems to be a pressing demand of the day.

*Itinerary Services*

Itinerary services of specialists like counsellor, special educator, audiologist or speech therapist seem to be a privilege for 30 per cent of schools only. But even in these schools, these specialists do not seem to be working in coordination. The purpose and the target groups for which these services are provided seem to have been forgotten. CSN are not provided enough time for redressal of their issues with these itinerants nor are the teachers helped by these specialists. This throws light on the magnitude of the issue of bringing in attitudinal changes in the school system, state policies and in the allocation of resources as also the urgency of efforts to coordinate and streamline all the different services already in place in the system.

*Counselling Services*

Counselling services in most of the schools are not adequate to address the needs of CSN and the parents, for various reasons stated by the Heads and the teachers, like the lack of interest of the parents, non-availability of such services in the schools etc. This calls for a re-look at such a service.

*Support to Teachers from Head*

Support from the Head is not forthcoming, with regard to problems faced by teachers in the classes vis-à-vis CSN. No suggestions, no redressal means, or dialoguing with CSN is done by the Head in most of these cases. This again calls for sensitizing the Heads of all schools in more effective ways and equipping them with modalities of tackling the issues, both directly with CSN and also through the teachers.

*Infrastructural Facilities*

Scheme of barrier free buildings, by way of constructing ramps and special toilet has been a great success in most of the schools. Hence, it seems a possibility that, similar efforts in the areas of service to other categories of challenged learners could also be worked out, like loops and group hearing aids in the classrooms etc for hearing challenged learners apart from individual hearing aids.

In the interpretive discussion presented above, it can be said that the system is definitely awakening to the needs of CSN. Infrastructural modifications are made, assessment camps are organized for assessment and provision of assistive aids to the needy, attempts to include inclusive education as part of in service teacher training programmes are evident, attempts to provide services of specialists like counsellor, special educator, speech therapists, audiologists etc have been initiated. The journey has begun, but we have a long way to go before we achieve our goal!

## Caveats and Challenges

The major caveats and challenges that emerged from the study are as below:

*Crowded Classes:* High strength of students in each class makes it rather difficult for the teachers to give any personal attention to the SNC.

*Inadequate Teacher Training:* Inadequate or absence of on-site support, inadequate practice oriented inputs from in-service training programmes and non-availability of suitable learning aids call for a major revamp of the teacher training programmes, especially the in-service training programmes focusing on the education of CSN in inclusive settings. Organising well planned itinerary services for on-site support and field intense resource mobilisation are as important as in-service training programmes, as informed by evidence from the field.

*Poor attendance* is an age old problem the system is trying to resolve, which is more acute in case of CSN. School going seems to be the easiest task at hand to be compromised whenever there is a need in the family. This issue is related to many other issues like poverty and cannot be addressed at just the school level.

*Absence of record of drop out:* The fact that schools generally do not maintain a record of drop out cases, nor of CSN who have dropped out or passed out indicates a lack of empathy and sensitivity of the system in general.

*Apathy of Parents:* The possibility of getting any participation from the parents in any aspect of the children's development seems to be totally non-existent.

*Lack of awareness among Heads and teachers:* The Heads and teachers are not aware of the nature and needs of CSN and the resultant transactional strategies to address their needs in learning.

*Lack of positive attitude among Heads and teachers:* The Heads and teachers do not reflect a positive attitude to including CSN in their schools/ classes. They seem to be just allowing them to be in the classes as they have no choice!

## Policy Implications

We live in a very ablest hegemony, there are some people who are very 'fine' and 'able', and others who are 'not so able', or are so called 'disabled'. Ability has great diversity: we need to recognize it, respect it and accept it. Ghai (2009). It is with this perspective can we approach the issues related to CSN.

Many of the issues of the education of the CSN are more acute reflections of the broader challenges in an education system which is grappling with issues of quality and drop out for children ***without*** specific needs even at the primary level. The issues are manifold in the context of education of CSN. Having infrastructural facilities and other resources independently does not facilitate inclusion. One of the most important impacting factor is the inclusive attitude of the teachers which can help and motivate CSN first to feel comfortably part of the group and then to try and learn.

While addressing such issues many multi pronged strategies would have to be designed from campaigning for awareness building among parents and community at large to revamping teacher education programmes. The bottom line is that students with special needs should have equitable access to opportunities that will guarantee successful outcomes in education, employment and community integration. But we are forced to ask ourselves, 'is the policy on inclusive education of CSN a compromising resolution of the conflict between a rights-based approach and that of economists and utilitarian approach as the resource allocation demanded by CSN for their education in special schools is much more than that of the regular children?'

*Disability is not just a state issue, but it is a state and society issue.* In the debates and discussions that will occur, teachers, administrators, other school personnel, law-makers, students with and without disabilities, and their parents must be cognizant of the responsibility of educating all students so they can reach their full potential for which attitudinal change is indispensable. Developing countries are attempting to blindly ape the advanced countries in matters related to education and other sectors. It is not sufficient for government officials to merely endorse international protocols of special needs education that have not been adequately researched or tested in developing countries. But, the challenge has to be fought with strategies to implement policies that are suitable to our field realities and improve the system by revamping all related sub-systems and services that have an impact on the success of the education of CSN.

## Conclusion

An important realization is that we (schools studied) are still working with a **medical model**, with all the gearing towards what is the 'deficit' in the learner. We have all data regarding the disability of the learner, and also have camps organised for the assessment of those CSN who have not been assessed. But, these data are reduced to records in safe custody and we are not very sure of what to do with these data. We do not know how these abilities and disabilities inform the classroom processes nor do we have the skills and knowledge required to bring in any transaction or assessment related adaptations in the classrooms. Above all, we are not yet ready to imbibe the spirit of inclusion as a philosophy nor do we have the right attitude towards children with special needs. Precisely, in an attempt at inclusive education of CSN, we have only reached a stage of integrating them, by 'letting them be' in the classes! We need to move from a medical model of focusing on disability to a **social model** or a rights based model by tuning to the modalities of responding to the needs of each CSN.

## REFERENCES

Abosi, O. & Koay, T. L. (2008). Attaining Development Goals of Children with Disabilities: Implications for Inclusive Education. *International Journal of Special Education.* 23 (3), 1-10.

Alur, M. (2001). Some Cultural and Moral Implications of Inclusive Education in India—a personal view. *Journal of Moral Education*, 30 (3).

Ghai, A. (2009) Views presented in a conference organized by Sambhavana in the University of Delhi on 'Disabled and the Right to Education: Stakeholders, State and Civil Society' (December, 2009).

(Sambhavana is n non- governmental organization)

People with Disabilities in India: From Commitments to Outcomes (2007). Human Development Unit, South Asia Region, The World Bank.

Topping, K. & Maloney, S. (2005) in, *Inclusive Education,* ed. Topping, K. & Maloney, S. Routledge Farmer: NY

UNESCO Regional Workshop on Inclusive Education: 'Getting All Children into School and Helping Them Learn', 19-21 October 2004, Bangkok, Thailand

http://www2.unescobkk.org/elib/publications/Inclusive_Edu (accessed on 14.10.2011)

# 5

# Teachers: Imperative Factor for Child Schooling at Elementary Level

*Jyotsna Ashok Amin and R.C. Patel*

In the post-Independence, Report of Kothari Commission (1964) has set three mission in the education; universalization of elementary education, vocationalisation of secondary education; and rationalization of higher education. If one looks on policy recommendations and programmes to improve quality of school education, lots of efforts have been made by the government. The National Policy on Education, NPE (1986) as revised in 1992, had emphasized the need for a substantial improvement in quality of education to achieve essential levels of learning. The Programme of Action (1992) stressed the need to lay down Minimum Levels of Learning (MLL) at Primary and Upper Primary stage. This need emerged from the basic concern that irrespective of caste, creed, location or sex, all children must be given access to education of comparable standards. The MLL strategy for improving the quality of elementary education was seen as an attempt to combine quality with equity. After the implementation of Sarva Shiksha Abhiyan (SSA), government has taken steps for institutional reforms, sustainable financing, community owner-ship and capacity building at elementary level. The main indicator of the quality of elementary education can be visualized in terms of its product – the learners' achievement both in scholastic and co-scholastic areas i.e. the performance in various subjects of study and habits, attitudes, values and life skills necessary for becoming a good citizen.

The factors associated with success in these areas, which relate to conditions of learning and learning environment, are also sometimes considered as indicators of quality of elementary education. Thus ensuring quality in the inputs and processes becomes necessary if quality achievement is aimed at. Ensuring quality in the inputs depends on those who provide inputs to the learners hence, teachers play indispensable role in the process of education. Any program, innovations or strategies be it competent enough, cannot succeed without the teachers because they are the one who executes it at grass root level. Many training programmes are being conducted by the authorities for capacity building of teachers at elementary level all over India even though certain inevitable issues still persist. Present paper attempts to highlight few commonly observe issues related to teachers which hampers the success at elementary level in Gujarat. Also it provides the profile of the teachers and status of the teachers at elementary level.

## Quality Concerns for Child Schooling

Quality issues in Elementary Education is revolve around the quality of infrastructure and support services, opportunity time, teacher characteristics and teacher motivation, pre-service and in-service education of teachers, curriculum and teaching-learning materials, classroom processes, pupil evaluation, monitoring and supervision etc. Indeed improvement of quality in these parameters and its sustenance is a matter of grave concern for the whole system of education. As per the guideline of SSA, out of fifteen issues few are mentioned below which are anyhow related to teachers of elementary level:

- Providing trained and committed teachers in all schools and really interested and oriented instructors for all non-formal education centers (EGS & AIE);
- Improving the quality of existing pre-service teacher education;
- Organizing quality in-service teacher education to all teachers on a periodical basis and with a follow up mechanism;
- Creating and sustaining teacher motivation;
- Re-organization of curriculum to imbibe local needs and incorporating the concerns of the National Curriculum Framework 2000;
- Improving teaching-learning processes to make them child centered, activity based, mastery learning oriented;
- Providing for remedial teaching and enrichment programmes at due occasions in all classrooms;

In order to achieve this decentralized management system with bottom to top approach is being used. Block Resource Centers and Cluster Resource Centers are established as per the norms and are in function under the guidance of DIETs. Efforts are made to identify teachers as resource person is through adoption of objective criteria. Teachers are being selected as resource persons and they interact with pedagogy experts and other teacher educators to develop useful learning approaches for children. Efforts to recognize the unique learning needs of children must be made. The effective interface of teachers and teacher educators, study tours and training in hard spots in teaching has helped in developing capacity among teachers for innovative practices. Wherever face to face interaction is not possible, then training by using multimedia packages like audio-video programmes, radio broadcast, teleconferencing, etc. are given to facilitate dissemination of innovative practices of one region to others. All the above mentioned are the illustrations of the efforts made by the government for the capacity building of the teachers TLM grant of ₹ 500 is given to every teacher per year to develop the teaching learning material.

**Teachers at Elementary Schooling in Gujarat**

Gujarat has been one of the leading states even before its establishment as a separate state to provide direction for elementary education in India during $19^{th}$ centuries. Flash statistics declared by Ministry of Human Resource Development (2010) about the elementary education in India has given some indications based on DISE.

- Literacy of Gujarat is around 70 per cent.
- Enrollment of students at primary and upper-primary level is 76.37 per cent and 71.97 per cent respectively.
- At present total 1,87,082 teachers are in position at elementary level in government schools of Gujarat against the total enrollment of 78,14,391 students at elementary level. Out of which 93.69 per cent teachers are professionally trained having minimum requirement for elementary teachers. 78.08 per cent of the teachers have received in-service training. 6.11 per cent teachers were involved in non-teaching activities during academic year 2008-09 for 13 days. Almost all the sectioned positions are filled in and, all over the state at present all the BRCCs and CRCCs are appointed and functioning for enhancing quality of education and trainings.
- Pupil teacher ratio is 32 at elementary level; at primary level it is 32 and at upper primary level it is 33.Avarage No. of teachers in one elementary school is 6.1.
- Average number of Classrooms per school is 5.2 in government elementary school.
- 1.42 per cent of Elementary schools have single teacher from which 3.47 per cent of are primary schools.
- Enrollment of schools having single teachers schools 2.02 per cent at primary level and that of 0.40 per cent at elementary level.

- 2.94 per cent of the primary schools have PTR more than 60 students per teachers and that of elementary school is 3.05 per cent.

Table 5.1 given below figure-outs the result of the above mentioned in terms of its retention and achievement in the examinations held during academic year 2009-10. The other side is the constant drop-out rate of students and failure of students in spite of the no detention policy.

**Table 5.1: Status of Gujarat in Elementary Education by 2009-10**

| *Sr. No.* | *Indicator* | | |
|---|---|---|---|
| 1. | Net Enrolment of students | Primary –85.80 per cent, Upper-primary–42.42 per cent | |
| 2. | Retention Rate | 84.59 per cent at elementary level | |
| 3. | Repetition Rate | Primary –5.83 per cent, Elementary level– 4.96 per cent | |
| 4. | Dropout Rate | 3.86 per cent –Elementary level | |
| 5. | Percent of students pass with more than 60 per cent | Primary level | Upper-primary level |
| | A. Boys | 62.05 | 67.29 |
| | B. Girls | 63.10 | 68.47 |

Previous lines have made it clear that government has dew concern about the Elementary Education and efforts are made to their best capacity. There are many factors which impede the mission of UEE one of which is the teacher. Largely all that is being plan is executed by the teachers in the classrooms. All the efforts are made for the capacity building of the teachers by the government. But the harsh reality is that if we check out the inputs provided by the teachers in the classrooms, we are at the first step only from where we have started.

## Status of Teachers at Elementary Schooling in Gujarat

In order to be elementary teacher in a government primary school, one needs to have a minimum of PTC degree. Earlier it was after 10th one was eligible to do PTC/ATD, now it has been raised to H.Sc. with any of the three discipline science, commerce and arts. Even after graduation also one can do PTC. In between if somebody has additional B.Ed. degree they are also eligible to be primary teachers and after five years they can be given promotion to the position of (Assistant Educational Inspector) A.E.I. at district level. This has created a wide variety of teachers at elementary level. Figure 5.1 indicates in details.

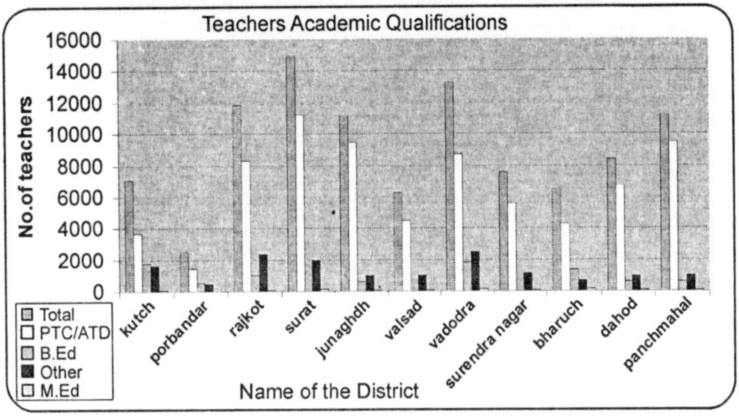


**Figure 5.1:** *Academic Qualification of the Regular Elementary Teachers in Selected Districts of Gujarat*

**A.** Teachers appointed with SSC PTC,

**B.** Teachers with HSC PTC-arts, science, commerce

**C.** Teachers with graduation with various subjects

**D.** Teachers with additional degrees like B. Ed. and M.Ed. that helps them in promotion later on.

Based on the qualifications teachers are recruited by the central selection committee at district level. At the time of recruitment of vacancies, new teachers are given choice of the schools as per their results of HSC board exams and PTC exams (40: 60) hence, they get the schools in the different areas may be unknown to them and far from their native place. In providing choices of the places regular teachers are given preference. In doing so, candidate with higher merit is given choices after the shifting of regular teachers at demanded places. Newly appointed teachers have to work on fixed pay of *Vidhya Sahayak* decided by the state government which ₹ 2500/- in case of Gujarat at the given place for the period of five year at least to be confirmed as a regular teacher. During this period services of the teachers may be terminated any time on unsatisfactory performance reported by the head teacher of the particular school. In the proceeding paragraphs few key factors identified are listed and attempt is made to discuss them in light of child schooling.

## Factors Affecting Teachers' Performance for Child Schooling

### *Academic Qualifications*

With the above mentioned conditions teachers are recruited and all of them are expected to teach the content of grade one to seven and all the subjects. Many of them have never studied science after their tenth.

Following table provide the same picture that majority of the teachers have had arts as their discipline at higher secondary level and very little knowledge about science.

**Table 5.2: Distribution of Teachers from 5 per cent of Schools from Selected Districts**

| *Qualification* *District* | *SSC, PTC* | *HSC Science* | *HSC/ Commarce* | *HSC/ Arts* | *ATD* | *Total* |
|---|---|---|---|---|---|---|
| Narmada | 20 | 05 | 01 | 28 | 05 | 59 |
| Panchmhals | 250 | 03 | 04 | 144 | | 425 |
| Kutch | 59 | 09 | 11 | 84 | - | 158 |

These teachers are given training on identifying hard spots at subject but they are not aware about the content and hence it results into poor achievement in terms of understanding of students. Even teachers having that subject knowledge of science find it difficult to teach science at seventh grade. Most of them are facing problem in teaching English and mathematics subject and reflected that teachers with specialization should be appointed. This can be applicable to any part of India.

*Commuting Teachers*

Teachers working as in the rural schools are either commuting or staying in the village only. It is seen from the statistics that majority of the teachers do not prefer to settle in the village and commute every day. This reflected that the government school cannot provide quality education to their wards and standards of life in rural area do not match with their status. In some cases the distance from the resident to Schools is more than 30-40 kms and daily they travel either by state transport or by private transport. In some cases the commuting cost exceeds their salary amount. Because they are commuting they do not come to the school on time and teaching suffers. Those who are commuting have their own family and hence they are always in the hurry to catch the bus and go home. In the case of female teachers situation is more serious that they have to finish of their routine at home, take care of child if any and managing the school timings. Even if they are in the school physically they remain busy mentally with their family. In the case of taking up some additional training they always find it difficult to attend it. Even after receiving training they neither can nor spare some time to think on it and implement it in the classrooms.

*Demographic Conditions*

*Seasonal Problems*: In the rural area at many places still schools are declaring holidays in some seasons because of the geographical conditions.

Schools situated in the remote and hilly areas where transport facility is not there and teachers and students have to walk down to reach to the school. In these situations even attendance in the school remains poor or many of the time; it is undeclared holidays in schools. During monsoon many of the schools are cut off from the town places and teachers cannot reach to schools on time or they do not want to take trouble to go to the schools. These are the places where hardly any ADI or monitoring team can go and even village people do not report such incidences.

*Local dialects*: Some time a teachers from a distant place or from another district is recruited in the schools and these teachers do not understand the local dialect of the students and communication suffers. Teachers have to learn the dialect of that locality and then translate the textbook content in to that and teach to the students. To help such teachers government has prepared dictionary of local dialect used by particular community in the remote areas and training is also provided. Even though teachers do not take much interest in the same and they face problems in dealing with students. The same problem is on the side students they cannot understand what the teacher is teaching in the class. Here teaching learning process is like one way communication not reaching to other end. Sometimes teachers try to teach in their dialect but ultimately they are to be evaluated with one standard question papers of regular language. Ultimately all these affect the result of the students.

*Family background of the teacher*: Many of the time teachers even if they are staying in the village cannot adjust to the social environment of the school because of his/her family and cultural back grounds. In some villages still untouchability, casteism and regionalism exist. Teachers having different backgrounds cannot adjust to it and fail to establish to have the conducive climate in the schools. Because of difference in the culture at home teacher fails to understand the feeling of students and cannot reach to them as the teacher from their background can do.

### *Academic Climate of the School*

Sometime in the comparison of what other teachers do there are teachers who not doing anything or stop doing the regular tasks. It depends on the work culture the principle has established in the schools. In many of the schools it is observed that few teachers are teaching multi grades and many are taking only one class even if teachers are available in the schools. In many schools it is observed that teachers are talking with the other teacher standing outside the class and students are not doing anything. Some female-teachers carry their house related work in the schools. The male teachers remain busy with the political gossiping or playing games on computers. Computers are remain as showpieces in the laboratory and teachers except playing games do not take trouble to learn the computer.

This is the scenario in majority of the schools situated in the remote areas where neither the parents nor the principal bothers about teachers teaching in the class or not.

*Mismatch in the Interest and Assigned Tasks*

Many of the time the teachers are not interested in some subjects and even though they are supposed to deal with them. Their interest and aptitude is different but may be because of family pressure or not getting admission in higher studies they have selected PTC for study and become primary teachers. These teachers are not yet mentally matured to deal with small children and they do not find it interesting. Teaching profession is not considered as a smart profession and losing status among youth. Majority of them have had their first choice something else and thus they cannot enjoy the teaching process. They find it difficult to create lively atmosphere in the classroom. Job satisfaction remains at their mind only and thus ultimately students do not find competent teachers and they also lack in their achievement. Many times if the teachers are enthusiastic they are not given proper tasks and somebody incompetent is given the task just because of seniority and juniors have to follow it. This gives dissatisfaction and unrest in teachers and they become inactive.

*Motivation from the Authority*

In the whole elementary level bottom to top approach is adopted and decentralization in the management is there. At many places teachers are given proper incentives and competitive spirit is developed. There teachers are doing good job but, many of the places teachers putting extra efforts are not being recognized and teachers involved in local politics are promoted as CRCs and BRCs and others feel neglected. Those who are new teachers they are bulled by the seniors, many of the time for their hard work and sincerity and in the absence of some motivation they also becomes like others. These teachers are getting salary of RS. 2500 i.e. the most de-motivating factor to the primary teachers.

*Attitude of the Teacher*

"There are ways if there is will". Majority of the teachers work fairly when they are in the initial five years probations. As soon as they get permanent they becomes lazy and inactive and this depends on attitude of the individual. There is no problem with those who are the born teachers, but those who joined teaching for earning purpose only they have made it in pitiable situations. Government has provided grant for preparing the Teaching Learning Material to every teacher of elementary schools in order to improve the teaching learning process and make it interesting and it was expected that teachers will utilize this TLM regularly in their classrooms. Every year they are getting five hundred rupees. Grants which are utilized but the TLM is still waiting to be used by the teachers. Every village schools are given toolkit-box for science teaching containing equipment of science experiments including microscope to even litmus papers. But teachers do not even open the box and use it in the classrooms no matter which discipline they belong either science or arts. They have a fear of spoiling the instruments thus they do not permit to students for using it. At primary level when they have no detention policy except in the case of attendance is less than 80 per cent, many students fail in exams and repeat the grades I and II. In this situation it is the teachers' inefficiency that they fail to catch the students' interest and they do not come to school.

*Commitment to the Profession*

Many of the teachers do not know about the professional ethics of the teaching profession and have very low self esteem and commitment level. This is the main cause affect their performance in the school. They fail to maintain the dignity of the teachers and involved themselves in malpractices. Many of the materials allocated by the government for the students are not made available to them. Mid day meal and its quality is also a question mark because of passive role of teachers.

## Conclusion

Teachers are the nation builders and makers of future citizens. It is said that in order to build a stronger construction the foundation should be strongest. Students of primary levels are passing through the foundation stage and it is believed that as you sow as you reap. Thus we will get the fruits accordingly. Teachers are the one who can give the flowers from the seed because child spends most of the child hood time in the school. It is from the primary level only citizenship and democratic behaviour is built up and thus teachers need to be of that calibre. An attitude can change the challenges in to opportunities. Only if teachers will change their attitude the mission of quality child schooling will get success.

## REFERENCES

Kothari D.S. (1966). Education Commission (1964-66) New Delhi: Ministry of Education.

Manu P. (1999). "Total Quality Management in Education", *University News*, 37 (32).

National Curriculum Framework For school Education (2005). NCERT, New Delhi.

MHRD (2010). "Elementary Education in India progress towards UEE: Flash statistics 2009-10 on retrieved on-04.01.2012 from http://infochangeindia.org/women/statistics/statewise-literacy-rates-in-india.html

Sharma R.N. (2002). "Problems of Education in India" Atlantic publishers: New Delhi.

# 6

# Purposes of School Social Work and Primary Education in India

*Ashish Agnihotri and Swati Bist*

The family unit and the school are the fundamental spaces for the growth of children. There are a lot of gaps in this relationship, within the school and family, and in their relations to each other and particularly to the specific requirements of students. There are fissures linking objective and actuality, between apparent need and accessible programs. In the vibrant multicultural environment around the child at present, there are gaps between various cultures and what education possibly will present to child. World wide it is a main concern that children grow and develop well and that schools support that needed development. However, aspirations are discontented, policies not succeed, and or else efficient programs fall short with certain students. School social workers practice in the "breathing space" where children, families, schools, kith and kin, and communities come across one another in a very complex way, where expectations can be unsuccessful; where gaps subsist: where education be able to break down. All over the world, schools are fetching the foremost institution for social growth and development. Schools are functioning to embrace those formerly excluded from the chance of learning; moving up values for educational effectiveness to prepare populace to contribute in a cosmopolitan world, leap collectively by communication, political, economic and social relations at fast pace.

The school social worker is suitable as a constructive professional to support children who are at periphery whether economically, socially, politically, or individually to play a part in this. Social workers work to put together the education progression efficient. To do this task, their essential focal point is working in corporation with parents on the student in transaction with a multifaceted school and home environment in furthering engagement. Education has befallen fundamental, not simply for everyone to cope with the difficulty of modern living, but also for national economic survival (Friedman, 2005). As a corollary of education's improved mission, an outcome based education organism is emergent.

This organism is exemplified by universal standards, supple ideas of education to rally these standards and higher values for education professionals to deal in a different way with diverse levels of requirements. Since children commence school with dissimilar dexterity, aptitude, attitude and resources, they do not begin with a same level playing field, and the burden of homogeneous standards on all children rationally directs to the need to modify resources to those who are further at possibility for failure.

School social workers practice in nearly all vulnerable components of the educational progression, and consequently their roles can be as multifarious as the realities they face. Practice respites on an extensive series of skills that are distinct and take shape throughout interactive collaboration. School social workers may work one on one with teachers, families, and children to deal with individual situations and needs in specific or generic manner. They happen to part of joint efforts to create schools safe for everyone. In maintaining the self-esteem and respect due any individual, the school needs to develop into a community of belongings and reverence. For example, social workers may toil with an entire school on developing positive policies and educational programs dealing with various types of harassments of the students. When the school comes to a decision to put into practice a zero tolerance policy, social workers are accessible to confer with teachers on execution and to work with sufferers and perpetrators of harassment. They may assist to develop a crisis intervention plan for the school with the principal, teachers, parents and staff. They may work with crisis team through alarming and violent incidents, working in diverse ways with individual student and teachers experiencing crisis and with the school populace. They may plan and develop violence prevention programs in the schools experiencing confrontations between students. The list continues through many variations.

**Rationale of School Social Work in Primary Schools**

School social workers have long been apprehensive in relation to children who are not proficient to make use of what education has to proffer them. More than the period of a century in India, schools have widened their task and compass on the way to becoming more inclusive and toward ensuring esteem for the individual differences of children. Therefore, social workers and numerous educators have drawn closer to contribute to analogous values within education system. Every person possesses inherent value; People have universal needs. Schools and families are environments where children should develop, discover their own dignity and worth, and get nearer to recognize their potential. Regrettably, the human impending of child is often pointlessly neglected in Indian scenario. The worlds of very young children, so filled of hope and aspirations, can also be taken over by odd and vague pictures of human value and of social relations in complexity. School social workers work with these tender minds and their school and family surroundings, assisting them to achieve responsibilities coupled with their education, growth, and development, and consequently to come to a fuller awareness of their inherent self-esteem, ability, and potential. The school social work role is developed from this purpose and these standards at large. It is not simply doing clinical or psychological kind of social work in a school but fit into place in larger sphere within a holistic frame work but in contemporary educational framework in India it is the most neglected area by policy makers across the nation.

The crucial focal point of the school social worker is the assemblage of teacher, parent, and child. The social worker must be proficient to relay to all aspects of the child's situation, but the fundamental skill underlying all of this is assessment, a methodical way of accepting and communicating what is happening and what is achievable. Edifice on assessment, the social worker build up a plan to assist the overall assemblage teacher and students in the classroom, parents, and others to work collectively to support the child in successfully carrying out the developmental ladder that lie down ahead.

The fundamental questions regarding school social work within Indian particularity are: What kind of the role of the school social worker should be in a particular school community? As India has its very diverse and plural populace and where are the finest spaces to intervene the units of concentration in these particular circumstances? Directed by the purposes and requirements of education and the learning practice, an efficient and inclusive school social work role can be settling within a school community nationwide; which would further result at significant level in primary education goals in India at larger scale. Thus, role, the key to the understanding of what the school social workers do, is a set of anticipated behaviors build by school social workers cooperatively with their school communities. In every school, the school social worker's role is developed by social workers with different counterparts, to do this, school social workers require to have visualization of what is feasible, acquire tools of analysis, be at ease with the processes of conciliation, and synchronize their interventions with the life of the school with standard values. They can build their role with others, assessing the requirements and main concern of the school community and perceptive what school social work can put forward.

**Table 6.1: Exemplar of School Social Work**

| *Social Work Values* | *Purpose of Social Work in Schools* |
|---|---|
| Acknowledgment of the worthiness and self-esteem of a human being as universal aspect | Every student is cherished as a human being despite the consequences of any distinctive attribute. |
| The right of self-determination or self-realization to every one | Every student should be permitted to share in the education process. |
| Reverence for individual capacity and acceptance for an individual's hope and desires to attain it | Individual disparity, difference in rate of learning should be acknowledged; interference should be intended at sustaining learning objectives. |
| The right of an individual to be dissimilarfrom each other and to be accordedadmiration for these disparity | Every child despite of caste, creed and socioeconomic distinctiveness, has an inherent right to equivalent treatment in the school community. |

## Emergence of School Social Work

The spotlight of school social work has followed the significant concerns of education. The troubles confronted by the education establishment over its long history have assortment from discrimination against specific social and economic groups, obliging migrant populace, absenteeism, and the catastrophic waste of human impending in poignant disturbances of childhood to problems regarding school disruption and protection, poverty, calamity, drugs, and AIDS. The first social workers in schools were hired in gratitude of the fact that conditions, whether in the family, the neighbourhood, or the school itself, that avert children from learning and the school from carrying out its mandate were the school's concern (Allen-Meares, Washington, & Welsh, 2000; Costin, 1978). School social work would depict its authenticity and its purpose from its capability to construct education work for groups of children who could not participate. Its olden times echo the sprouting consciousness in education, and in society, of groups of children for whom education has not been effective: poor, migrants, economically and socially oppressed, delinquent, and specially challenged. It represents its purpose from the requirements and in due course the rights of these groups as they interfaced with the institution of education and face up to the anticipation that they should accomplish their potential. In all circumstances, as school social workers definite their roles, there was a match of the social work standpoint its knowledge, values, and skills with the undertaking and mandate of the school.

During the twentieth century, schools wide-reaching; broadened their task and range toward larger inclusion and high opinion for the individual disparity of children. The opening of obligatory school attendance laws in U.S.A. around from 1895 through 1918, noticeable a major move in philosophies and policies governing American education in a holistic way. This would ultimately become a philosophy of inclusion. Education, no longer for the privileged, was for all and sundry an indispensable part of grounding for modern life. A half century later, the incredibly first time in olden times, the U.S. Supreme Court endorsed that education is a constitutional right, which, if accessible to any, must be obtainable to all on an equal basis and this acumen further reflected in Right to Education Act, 2009 of India. In the evident light of current phenomenon there is severe pondering that if education is a principal instrument in serving the child to fiddle with normally to this complex environment, it is doubtful that any child may plausibly be expected to do well in life if he is denied the chance of an education. The opportunity of an education, where the state has undertaken to endow with it to any, is a right, which must be made obtainable to all on equal conditions.

The conviction that education, if available to any, should be obtainable uniformly to all was also keyed up by the evolving awareness of individual disparity among students and the requirements, certainly the responsibility of the school, to become accustomed curriculum to this difference. The preliminary plunge of education in a modern society would be to homogenize curriculum, and thus the learning procedure, into one most excellent way to be taught and one set of subjects to be learned. The modern school was prearranged by a prescribed curriculum, consistent testing, and the grade system. Students had to robust into this agreed curriculum and a very new learning process. The dilemma is that not a bit of this equivalence of learners, knowledge, and the education process counterpart the real world. Learners are dissimilar; Learning is mutually an individual process and a relational progression. Any program of study is potentially assorted: it transform as knowledge changes. For students to study optimally, the repercussion of this distinction must be recognized. Testing and teaching research recognized this divergence, but actual change would come gradually. The system of education within the typical of the grade system ultimately became rather more individualized. Children with disabilities acknowledged individualized education programs with goals, anticipated learning process, and educational assets customized to their needs. The association to individualize education for all children in the perspective of values of achievement continues to be one of the innermost issues in education. Philosophy of inclusion and high opinion for individual diversity persist to profile the practice of education and offer the starting point for the role of the school social work in an education system particularly to developing countries like India which have diverse society.

**The Historical Development of School Social Work**

School social work set in motion during the school year 1906–1907 concurrently in New York, Boston, Hartford (Costin, 1969a), and Chicago (McCullagh, 2000). These workers were not taken into service by the school system but worked in the school under the funding of other organizations and civil society groups. In New York, it was a settlement house that pays for the workers. Their rationale was to work in a range of projects involving the school and communities of new immigrants, encourage understanding and communication (Lide, 1959). In Boston, the Women's Education Association funded "visiting teachers" who would work linking the home and the school. In Hartford, Connecticut, a psychology clinic formulated a program of visiting teachers to lend a hand the psychologist in obtaining social histories of children and put into practice of the clinic's treatment plans and suggestions (Lide, 1959). Similarly in Chicago, Louise Montgomery promoted a social settlement kind of program at the Hamline School that presented a wide range of services to the Stockyards District community (McCullagh, 2000). This unheralded experimentation projected a great deal which later resulted in development of school based services for the whole community. In many ways these miscellaneous early programs enclosed in irregular and in seminal form all the rudiments of afterward school social work practice. Over the following century, the apprehension of inclusion and acknowledgment of individual disparity, the notion of education as a relational process, and the developing task of the schools would outline the role of the school social worker.

In 1913 in Rochester, New York, the Board of Education hired visiting teachers for the first time and the school's commitment to employ visiting teachers was an acceptance of both the expansion mission of education and the prospect that social workers could be part of that mission. In explanatory to the appointments, the Rochester Board of Education distinguished that in the child's surroundings outer the schools there are forces that frequently prevent the school in its endeavours to educate student. The school was now lengthening and individualizing its mission, endeavouring to congregate its tasks for the "overall welfare of the child," and maximize "cooperation between the home and the school" (Julius Oppenheimer, cited in Lide, 1959).

Afterwards, three years later in 1916 at the National Conference of Charities and Corrections, an explanation of school social work appeared in the presentation of Jane Culbert. This explanation would focus on the environment of the child and the school, relatively than on the individual child. The school social worker's role was focused on understanding the school and the child's out of school life; enhancement the teacher's acquaintance of the child so that teacher may be able to teach the child in a holistic way; supporting the school to be familiar with the life of the vicinity, in order that it may educate the children to the existence to which they look forward. Secondly the visiting teacher read between the lines to parents the demands of the school and give details the particular difficulty and needs of the child" (Culbert, 1916, p. 595). The definition is abounding with concepts of education as a complex, relational process in the school community process school social workers could efficiently sustain in the wellbeing of children. Many of these notions would uncover further development in education over the century: inclusion, respect for individual disparity, and education as a progression taking place in the classroom, family and community. Culbert's account of role would be developed by Julius Oppenheimer in the school, family, community triangulation (Lide, 1959). From his study of 300 case studies by school social workers and visiting teachers collectively, he illustrated thirty two nucleus functions that he considered to be key to the role of the school social worker. School social workers would assist in the restructuring of school administration and practices by providing verification of critical circumstances causal school difficulties for students and by narrating out where changes were required (Allen-Meares, 2006; Allen-Meares et al., 2000).

In 1920, the National Association of Visiting Teachers was organized its foremost meeting in New York City (McCullagh, 2000). Concern was expressed about the organization, administration, and role definition of visiting teachers (Allen-Meares, 2000). This organization, which afterward became the American Association of Visiting Teachers, would publish a journal, the Bulletin. The Bulletin was the place in which the writing and the thinking of this embryonic field of practice emerged during these years. As a consequence of the influence of the mental hygiene movement of the day, there was a gradual shift in focus from the home and school environment to the individual schoolchild and that child's needs.

In 1949, Florence Poole illustrated a supplementary developed justification for school social work practice derivative from the right of every child to an education. Student who could not use what the school had to propose were "children who are being denied, obscure though the cause may be, nevertheless denied because they are unable to use fully their right to an education" (Poole, 1959, p. 357). It was the school's accountability to offer them impressive that would help them to assistance from an education. Education would need to change to assist children who were "having some particular difficulty in participating beneficially in a school experience" (Poole, 1959, p. 357). Her underlying principle would in due course mark a change in the debate of the school social work role. School social work would be indispensable to the schools' facility to bring about their purpose: "At the present time we no longer see social work as a service appended to the schools. We see one of our most significant social institutions establishing social work as an integral part of its service, essential to the carrying out of its purpose, we recognize clarity in the definition of the services as a social work service" (Poole, 1949, p. 454). She saw the precision and distinctiveness of social work service as coming from the societal purpose of the school. The worker "must be able to determine which needs within the school; can be appropriately met through school social work service. She must be able to develop a method of offering the service which will fit in with the general organization and structure of the school, but which is identifiable as one requiring social work knowledge and skill. She must be able to define the service and her contribution in such a way that the school personnel can accept it as a service, which further contributes to the major purpose of the school" (Poole, 1949, p. 455). Florence Poole's come close to practice was put together on the consideration of the mission of the school, the knowledge and skill of social work, and the worker's professional accountability to establish what requirements to be done and to develop an suitable program for doing it. Her formation, focused on the potentially prosperous interface of social work methods and the assignment of the school, was all together freer to use an assortment of methods to accomplish multifaceted personal, familial, and institutional goals. Poole eventually shifted the centre of attention from the problem learner who could not adjust and become accustomed to the school to student and schools adapting to each one other in the framework of every child's right to an education.

The settings that hinder with the student's capacity to unite with the educational system are various. Therefore, the functions of the school social worker would be bendable and broad ranging, developed in each school by come across with the tangible tribulations and requirements of the school community. The rudiments of this stumble upon have remained the identical over numerous years, while the role has developed and school social workers have responded to shifting surroundings. New purposes would become known on the widespread considerations sketched out by Florence Poole's vision. During the late 1960s and following years there occurred a transformed awareness in developing theory and practice in areas such as school social work.

During the final three decades of the twentieth century, the inclusive and individualizing missions of the schools were extended in answer to the acknowledgment of the right of children with disabilities and special needs to a free fitting education; and recent concerns around violence, sexual harassment, and bullying in schools at larger spheres. Education is becoming product and evidence based (Kratochwill & Shernoff, 2003). There is a public policy stress on high professional qualifications that is engaging toward specialization in school social work. In accordance with international standards practices, nations are setting standards for highly qualified school social workers and introducing post masters mentorships for more permanent certification for highly qualified school professionals in schools (Constable & Alvarez, 2006).

### Servitude to Child

Society spaces a serious liability on schools and families. Schooling is not merely a process of teaching and learning, but of prepare children for the future. Schools are the medium for aspiration and hope, not only for children who may be conventional effortlessly for peripheral expectations, but for every child. Responsibilities are positioned on the school, parent, and child to compose the educational process work so that each child who goes to school may fulfil his or her potential for growth. Schools require being fretful for every child whose coping faculty is not well harmonized with the burden and resources of the educational institution. At one time or other, any human being could be vulnerable. In accumulation, particular groups have borne sure burdens within society. Children come to school with hopes from society, and sometimes from the school itself. Conceivably they experience that because of certain defining characteristics, such as gender, caste, disability, ethnicity, or socioeconomic status, they cannot have the same aspirations as others, or objective conditions, such as poverty, will surely prevent them from achieving their aspirations. The influence of education, and many of the values that drive it, can refute these messages.

### Realm of School Social Work

### The School Community Frame

School is conceptualized as a community of family units and school human resources occupied in the educational progression. The educational process is lively and extensive which involves children, families, and an institution. It is the context for school social work; school is no longer viewed as a building or a set of classrooms in which teachers and students work together in learning. The school community, no longer simply bounded by boundaries, encompasses all those who take on in the educational process. As community it has varied tangible roles; individuals fit into these communities in very dissimilar ways. Parents and families have association through their children. Teachers and other school staff are members with responsibility to parents, children, and the society. Portrayal on each person's capability, the school social worker focuses on making the educational process work to the full scope. Therefore, school social workers work with parents, teachers, students, and administrators on behalf of children. The accomplishment of the process depends on the combined and individual participation; the social worker assist the school community function as a real community so that personal, family, and community resources can be exposed and used to meet children's fundamental growth developmental needs.

The school is swiftly fetching the place of organization of all services to children and families. As long as it had been taken for granted that school would be inaccessible from the home, one part of the role of the school social worker has been to distance the periphery between home and school. This has taken place since the origin of school social work in the early twentieth century (Litwak & Meyer, 1966). Schools have in general operated in comparative isolation from their ingredient families, each protecting its functioning from "interference" from the other. This isolation is, of course, counterproductive in circumstances of vulnerability or problems. There is a call for someone like the school social worker to cover, and even face, these limitations.

**The Social Milieu**

The association of school social work to its school and community framework is indispensable for the development of desired education system in India. The current Indian legal and social policy is inadequate in the context for school social work and the role of the school social worker in schools there is severe policy development required in India. There has been an erosion of state welfare systems and the supports government provides to families. As Indian government policies shift toward "market" approaches, it seems that the societal protections normally associated with childhood are declining.

Many families are deteriorating at large whereas risks to children are increasing. High rates of suicide, addiction, violence against children, sexual deviance amongst children, teen pregnancy, AIDS, are among these risks, to some extent created and in any case continuous by a laissez-faire outlook linked with the reigning free market way of life. Some of the menace generated by the market force and the broader social system may be cushioned through amplification of institutions at the local level through schools and homes. In the face of these problems schools have continued their century old expedition, such as for greater inclusion in the educational mainstream of formerly excluded groups of children. The changes that have taken place in special education over the past thirty years are particularly important and reflect the possible relations between school policy and the school social worker's role. More recently, school reform experience globally has been bringing with it increased expectations for children. Yet no progress can be made on school reform if the problems that accompany poverty and socioeconomic class that children are at risk and will not fulfill their potential without institutional, community, and family supports are not dealt with (Mintzies & Hare, 1985). Impoverished school working with impoverished families generally achieve at rates considerably lower than their more privileged neighbours (Biddle, 1997).

## Role of School Social Worker

The school social worker's role is multi-faceted assessment and discussion within the school team. There is straight work with children and parents individually and in groups and program and policy development for child welfare in a holistic manner. A list of the tasks that entry level school social workers perform in their day-to-day professional roles provides evidence of the complexity of school social work which fell along five job dimensions as follows:

1. Relationships with and services to children and families.
2. Relationships with and services to teachers and school staff.
3. Services to other school staff.
4. Community services.
5. Administrative and professional tasks (Dennison, 1998).

Further research on these roles, tasks, and skills found four areas of school social work to be both very important and frequently addressed:

1. Consultation with others in the school system and the teamwork relationships that make consultation possible.
2. Assessment applied to a variety of different roles in direct service, in consultation, and in program development.
3. Direct work with children and parents in individual, group, and family modalities.
4. Assistance with program development in schools (Constable et al., 1999).

A key skill, the foundation of all other areas, is assessment. Assessment is a systematic way of understanding what is taking place in relationships in the classroom, within the family, and between the family and the school. The social worker looks for units of attention places where intervention will be most effective. Needs assessment, a broader process, provides a basis for program development and policy formation in a school.

It is often a more formal process that utilizes many of the tools of research and is geared toward the development of programs and policies that meet the needs of children in school.

## Conclusion

In schools, social workers often serve as the link between students' families and the school, working with parents, guardians, teachers, and other school officials to ensure students reach their academic and personal potential. In addition, they address problems such as misbehaviour, truancy and advise teachers on how to cope with difficult students. Increasingly, school social workers teach workshops to entire classes. School social workers provide social services and assistance to improve the social and psychological functioning of children and their families and to maximize the well being of families and the academic functioning of children. They may assist single parents, arrange adoptions, or help find foster homes for neglected, abandoned, or abused children. Some specialize in services for senior citizens. These social workers may run support groups for the children of aging parents; advice elderly people or family members about housing, transportation, long-term care, and other services; and coordinate and monitor these services. It is important to understand the nature of Indian education policy as it is blind towards school social work practice in the nation at large. The involvement with education and schooling creates a natural focus on research, policy, and program development as practice. From basic practice skills of assessment and consultation in the framework of ecological systems theory flow a wide range of possible interventions. These are developed with teachers, pupils, families, and groups. They involve clinical practice, consultation and teamwork, coordinating and integrating services, developing inclusion plans, dealing with crisis and safety issues in the school, and developing mediation and conflict resolution, each with its own sources of theory. For many school systems, these standards will reinforce current practices. For others, they will provide a challenge and a goal to be achieved. For school social workers, they both validate the uniqueness and diversity of school social work as a specialty practice area and affirm the value of school social work in enabling students to achieve maximum benefits from their educational experiences.

## REFERENCES

Abbott, E. (1942). Social welfare and professional education (pp. 12-15). Chicago: University of Chicago Press.

Alderson, J. (1974). Models of school social work practice. In R. Sarri & F. Maple (Eds.), *The school in the community* (pp. 57–74). Washington, DC: National Association of Social Workers.

Allen-Meares, P. (1999). The contributions of social workers to schooling, revisited. In R. Constable, S. McDonald, & J. Flynn (Eds.), *School social work: Practice, policy, and research perspectives* (4th ed., pp. 24–31). Chicago: Lyceum Books.

Allen-Meares, P. (2006). One hundred years: A historical analysis of social work services in the schools. *School Social Work Journal*, 30 (3), 24–43.

Allen-Meares, P., Washington, R. O., & Welsh, B. L. (2000). Social work services in schools (pp 34-37). Boston: Allyn & Bacon.

American Association of Social Workers. (1974). Social casework: Generic and specific: A report on the Milford Conference. Washington, DC (pp. 76-77), National Association of Social Workers. (Reprint of 1929 edition)

Anlauf-Sabatino, C. (1982). Consultation and school social work practice. In R. Constable & J. Flynn (Eds.), *School social work: Practice and research perspectives* (pp. 271–281). Homewood, IL: Dorsey.

Bartlett, H. (1959). The generic-specific concept in social work education and practice. In A. E. Kahn (Ed.), *Issues in American social work* (pp. 159–189). New York: Columbia University Press.

Bartlett, H. (1971). The common base of social work practice (pp. 59-62). New York: National Association of Social Workers.

Biddle, B. J. (1997). Foolishness, dangerous nonsense, and the real correlates of state differences in achievement. Phi Delta Kappan, 79 (1), 8–13. Brown v. Board of Education of Topeka, 347 U.S. 483 (1954).

Chavkin, N. (1993). The use of research in social work practice (pp. 91-92). Westport, CT: Praeger.

Constable, R., & Alvarez, M. (2006). Moving into specialization in school social work. *School Social Work Journal*, 30 (3), 116–131.

Constable, R., Kuzmickaite, D., Harrison, W. D., & Volkmann, L. (1999). The emergent role of the school social worker in Indiana. *School Social Work Journal*, 24 (1), 1–14.

Constable, R., & Montgomery, E. (1985). A study of role conceptions of the school social worker. *Social Work in Education*, 7 (4), 244–257.

Costin, L. (1969a). A historical review of school social work. *Social Casework*, 50, 439–453.

Costin, L. (1969b). An analysis of the tasks in school social work. *Social Service Review*, 43, 274–285.

Costin, L. (1972). Adaptations in the delivery of school social work services. *Social Casework*, 53, 350.

Costin, L. (1973). School social work practice: A new model. *Social Work*, 20 (2), 135–139.

Costin, L. (1978). Social work services in schools: Historical perspectives and current directions (Continuing Education Series No. 8). Washington, DC: National Association of Social Workers.

Culbert, J. (1916). Visiting teachers and their activities. In Proceedings of the National Conference on Charities and Corrections (p. 595). Chicago: Heldman Printing.

Dennison, S. (1998). School social work roles and working conditions in a southern state. *School Social Work Journal*, 23 (1), 44–54.

Friedman, T.L. (2005). It's a flat world, after all. *New York Times Magazine*, from http://newyorktimes.com/magazine

Germain, C. (2006). An ecological perspective on social work in the schools. In R. Constable, Massat, R. C., S., McDonald, & J. P. Flynn (ed.), 2004. *School Social Work: Practice, Policy and Research* (6th ed., pp. 28-39). Chicago: Lyceum Books.

Gordon, W. E. (1969). Basic constructs for an integrative and generative conception of social work. In G. Hearn (Ed.), *The General Systems Approach: Contributions Toward an Holistic Conception of Social Work* (pp. 5-11). New York: Council on Social Work Education.

Herbert, B. (2007, October 2). Our schools must do better. *New York Times*, from http://www.nytimes.com/2007/10/2/opinion/02herbert

Joint NASW-CSWE Task Force on Specialization. (1979). Specialization in the social work profession (NASW Document No. 79-310-08). Washington, DC: National Association of Social Workers.

Kratochwill, T. R., & Shernoff, E. S. (2003). Evidence-based practice: Promoting evidence based interventions in school psychology (WCER Working Paper No. 2003-13).

Madison: Wisconsin Center For Educational Research. Retrieved August 8, 2004, from http://www.wcer.wisc.edu/Publications/workingPapers/Working_Paper_No_ 2003_13.pdf

Lambert, C., & Mullally, R. (1982). School social work: The congruence of task importance and level of effort. In R. Constable & J. Flynn (Eds.), *School Social Work: Practice and Research Perspectives* (pp. 72-99). Homewood, IL: Dorsey.

Lide, P. (1959). A study of the historical influences of major importance in determining the present function of the school social worker. In G. Lee (Ed.), *Helping the Troubled School Child: Selected Readings in School Social Work.* New York: National Association of Social Workers.

McCullagh, J. (2000). School social work in Chicago: An unrecognized pioneer program. *School Social Work Journal*, 25 (1), 1–14.

Mintzies, P., & Hare, I. (1985). The human factor: A key to excellence in education (pp87-89). Silver Spring, MD: National Association of Social Workers.

Poole, F. (1949, December). An analysis of the characteristics of the school social worker. *Social Service Review*, 23, 454–459.

Poole, F. (1959). The social worker's contribution to the classroom teacher. In G. Lee (Ed.), Helping the troubled school child: Selected readings in school social work. New York: National Association of Social Workers.

# 7

# Schooling of Slum Children

## *A Case Study of NGO Run Schools in Delhi*

***Pankaj Das and Shilpi Bhaskar***

One of the important international conventions, i.e. the UN Convention on the Rights of the Child (1989), strongly advocates for the protection of children's rights, to help meet their basic needs and to expand their opportunities to reach their full potential. It spells out the basic human rights that children everywhere have: the right to survival; to develop to the fullest; to protection from harmful influences, abuse and exploitation; and to participate fully in family, cultural and social life. The four core principles of the Convention are non-discrimination; devotion to the best interests of the child; the right to life, survival and development; and respect for the views of the child. The Convention protects children's rights by setting standards in health care; education; and legal, civil and social services. Henceforth, all the countries across the world have committed themselves to protect and ensure the rights of children residing in any part of the country urban or rural. With the effective strategies for Education for All (EFA), the government have even a much crucial and significant onus for its citizens, in particular the future citizens, the youth. More or less universalization of elementary education in India has been one of the effective strategies of the government to achieve the EFA since long. Also, access to primary education has been legally accepted as a human right for more than five decades now. But the irony of the fact is that even after the government's many successive programmes and policies to achieve the goals of EFA, it still raises many questions like which sections of the society are entitled to get the education as a fundamental right and how? Whether the government ensures that all the children from different social ladders, regions, religious communities and different classes are equally provided the basic rights to education among themselves? The answers to these questions many not have direct and straight forward answers but it points out one basic fact that in India great emphasis is laid on the policy statements, it does not necessarily and effectively covers the marginalized or the deprived groups at the time of its implementation (Sudarshan, 2000). Among the many vulnerable sections of child population in India, one of the most neglected is the population in the urban slum. The problem is acute in the slum areas in almost all mega urban centres including Delhi. Slums are a universal phenomenon and exist in practically all the cities across the world. Delhi alone has approximately 1,100 big and small unauthorized settlements comprising six lakh jhuggies forming various clusters of slums. As far as the reports of three surveys conducted in the national capital of India have found that nearly quarter of a million children living in slums do not go to schools. The findings have also highlighted the problems of unemployment, poor health and lack of civic facilities among the city's slum dwellers. India's slum population was projected to rise to 93.06 million by 2011, or 7.75 per cent of the total population, say a report of an expert committee set up by the housing and urban poverty alleviation ministry (Chauhan, 2009). Thus, a quarter of a million of Delhi's children, living in the slums or on the streets do not go to school poses a big hurdles to achieve the goals of Education for All.

**An Overview of the Status of Education in Slums**

There have been many studies on education of all levels in India but qualitative studies concentrating on the urban slum areas and education of slum children are very rare. Constitutionally and legally every child deserves education as a part of human rights. But the fact is that enrolment of students in primary schools in slum areas it is very low in comparison to the enrolment of children in Delhi as a whole. Even if they do enroll the dropout rate is very high. A number of studies in urban slums have substantiated the marginal role of formal schooling in the lives of slum children especially girl children. A Delhi study (Karlekar 1987) among the Balmikis, a sub-caste of the North Indian Bhangis or sweepers found that as girls were expected ultimately to combine housework with marriage; schooling was of little consequence. In a Bombay slum it was found by A.R. Desai and S.D. Pillai (1972) that illiteracy was three times as high among the women and girls than among men. Women in migrant *bastis* in Delhi were prepared to send their daughters to primary school for few years but hoped that their sons would finish school (A.M. Sing and A. DeSouza 1980). Research in India has been conducted by plethora of organization, non-governmental organizations who have been working to bring definite changes in education of deprived groups of our society.

In this situation Deepalaya, an NGO in Delhi comes into action, which has been running schools for such slum dropouts through sustained efforts to bring them back into the education fold. Deepalaya as a non-governmental organization derives its rationale for various programmes from such startling facts.

Deepalaya strives to educate the underprivileged section of the society through formal and non-formal education especially the slum children. In Delhi region, Deepalaya has five formal schools namely Deepalaya School Gole Kuan (DSGK), Deepalaya School Kalkaji Extension (DSKE), Ramditti J.R.N. Deepalaya School (RJRND), Deepalaya School Sanjay Colony (DSSC) and Deepalaya School Gusbethi (DSG). Today, Deepalaya has established 337 educational centers where 50, 000 beneficiaries are educated through formal and non-formal education. Deepalaya is accredited to National Open School for both academic and vocational purposes.

### Case Study of Deepalaya School Gole Kuan

Out of these schools in Delhi, *Deepalaya School Gole Kuan (DSGK)* was chosen as a case study to explore the schooling of the slum learners in India. The Gole Kuan is a slum in Okhla Industrial Area, Phase 1. In the year 1990 Deepalaya started the Gole Kuan Project for the upliftment of the slum dwellers. The low literacy levels pointed to the urgent need of education among the slum dwellers. Deepalaya School at Gole Kuan was set up to meet this need. The formal school programme is a follow on to the Gole Kuan Project. Gole Kuan also currently runs various other projects such as Vocational Training Centre, Disability Unit, Computer Training Unit, Health and formulation of Self Help Groups and other Community Organisations. The school conducts classes from LKG to VIII with a special focus on the girl child. It has strength of 329 students. Out of which there are 154 girls and 175 boys.

Currently, there are 310 students attending the school, who are taught by 14 teachers. A point to note is that a student teacher ratio of 22:1 in this school is a plus point that even most private schools are not able to provide. This ensures more scope for individual attention to the students. Of the 310 children studying in the school 177 are sponsored by corporate or individuals. Even girls are sponsored more by the corporate and individuals than the boys in this school and the selections of sponsorship of the learners are based on the criteria of the poorest economic background of the learners among the total learners.

The Table 7.1 indicates the distribution of slum learners in gender wise as well as sponsorship wise.

**Table 7.1: Distribution of Slum Learners in Gender-wise As Well As Sponsorship-wise**

| | *Total No. of Slum learners in Sponsorship and Non-Sponsorship wise* | | | | | |
|---|---|---|---|---|---|---|
| | *Sponsored* | | | *Non Sponsored* | | |
| *Classes* | *Girls* | *Boys* | *Total* | *Girls* | *Boys* | *Total* |
| LKG | 4 | 0 | 4 | 16 | 11 | 27 |
| UKG | 12 | 3 | 15 | 6 | 18 | 24 |
| I | 11 | 4 | 15 | 9 | 23 | 32 |
| II | 12 | 10 | 22 | 1 | 11 | 12 |
| III | 19 | 13 | 32 | 1 | 3 | 4 |
| IV | 15 | 9 | 24 | 5 | 8 | 13 |
| V | 16 | 7 | 23 | 0 | 5 | 5 |
| VI | 11 | 7 | 18 | 3 | 11 | 14 |
| VII | 3 | 7 | 10 | 0 | 10 | 10 |
| VIII | 5 | 9 | 14 | 0 | 11 | 11 |
| Total | 109 | 68 | 177 | 45 | 107 | 152 |

## Unique Features of the School

- In 1999, when Deepalaya decided to establish a school in Gole Kuan, there was some amount of resistance from the community. They cited reasons such as fees being beyond their means and non-recognition of the school as an issue for not sending their children to school. Deepalaya mobilised these communities through surveys, door-to-door campaigns and promotional material that educating children, especially girls was extremely important for their own welfare. Adult education classes were started to encourage the community following which many started sending their children to school. To this date Deepalaya teachers work within the community exhorting the parents to send their children to school. Those community members who are able to bring in large numbers of children to school are rewarded with gifts. Another significant achievement for the project was ownership by the community of the education programme when they donated 6 rooms for running the school within the community.
- Over time significant changes have been observed in the community ever since Deepalaya has been in touch with the lives of the people of Gole Kuan. Community awareness about the education of the girl child has increased significantly. The average age of girls getting married young has risen from about 16 to 19 now.

- Deepalaya encourages these girls to take up vocational training provided within the school and improve their chances of earning a livelihood.
- Standards of primary education too have improved as more and more out of school children have been brought within the education fold
- The project expanded to include *disadvantaged groups* such as differently-abled and those from minority communities deprived of education.
- *English Access class* is a special programme in collaboration with *American Library* forms an important part of students who are 13 years of age. The students are shortlisted on the basis of a written exam in English. The qualified students are then send on a weekly basis (Monday, Wednesday and Friday after the school gets over) to Deepalaya School-Kalkaji Extension where the students are taught using different aids so as to improve their language skills (listening, reading, speaking and writing). In the month of February, the learners were shown a movie. On the basis of watching the movie, they were asked to draw something. The teacher then discussed each drawing in detail. Also, they were asked to form a story of what they drew. In another activity, the students were shown a collage. Opinion was gathered on the basis of the collage they saw. *These activities also stimulate the imagination of the learners.* Currently, 13 students from this school are attending the English Access classes. Rock Jam live at AES Deepalaya has been rewardingly associated with the American Embassy School (AES) for a number of years now. Under a reach out programme, AES students and their parents have been teaching English and Maths to 40 students of Deepalaya School, Golekuan.
- The school also contributed in Deepalaya pioneering measure of becoming the first NGO to have its schools release a fully fledged school magazine—*Deep Thoughts*
- There are many achievers who are product of this school. One of the faculty teachers is alumni of this school. Other includes Harender who is working in a computer firm. Another student Pooja has completed her B.Ed, Munna is doing BCA along with part time Job. There are two project teachers working in the same school.
- Some of the students from the Muslim community also go to Madrasas on Fridays where they learn Arabic and also learn

about their religion besides attending classes in the school.

- The school conducts parent teacher meetings regularly every month which is well attended by about 90 per cent of the parents. During these meetings, the progress of the children, are discussed with the parents with a view to enhance their academic performance. Apart from these meetings the teachers make regular house visits and also meet parents at school for any special needs of the child.
- The school follows National Council for Educational Research and Training (NCERT) syllabus in all its classes. The children study to acquire Certifications of Open Basic Education (OBE), conducted by the National Institute of Open Schooling (NIOS), approved by the Ministry of Human Resource Development (HRD), Government of India in classes III, V and VIII. Besides the NIOS exams, the school conducts three terminal examinations over the year. The final examinations are conducted in the month of March. The children also undertake weekly tests to prepare themselves for the terminal examinations.
- The school has a well-equipped library with 565 books. In the year 2006 American Centre Library donated 364 books to the school. Many of these books which comprise of comics, stories and autobiographies cater to children from LKG to Class VIII. Reading these books, have opened a whole new world of knowledge for these young inquisitive minds. The school also tied up with Springdales School who send a mobile library to the slum every Monday to encourage good reading habits among children.

## Pedagogical Practices: Inside Story from the Classrooms

The formal school which runs classes from LKG (Lower Kindergarten) to Class VIII operates in two overlapping shifts from 7.50 AM to 2 PM and from 1.00 PM to 5.00 PM. This is because the school is unable to accommodate all the children enrolled in one shift due to paucity of space. The *medium of instruction* is supposed to be English as per the objective of Deepalaya of establishing English medium school. But it was found that the teachers were using both Hindi and English as medium of instruction. When the research scholar glanced through the notebook of some students of grade 2, it was seen that the more exercises and practices were in Hindi than in English. Also, when the research scholar interacted with class 2 students they were unable to answer to the question in English, but they were comfortable in answering the same in Hindi.

The class 2 students recited the same Hindi poem that they had learnt in grade 1. No English poem was recited. One of the students was asked to convert number 9390 that was written in his class notebook into word. But the student was unable to do so even when the number was written by himself in the notebook, though in English. This speaks volumes to the present educational status of the slum learners in the school.

In one of the instances of the field study it was observed many underling factual matters with the informal conversations with the class six students. The class had more boys than girls. Interestingly, 3 students had left the government school so as to study in this school on the pretext of quality education. Also, in the same class many of the students were paying tuition fees for studying subjects like Mathematics and English. They candidly discussed the advantages of going to tuition. Although they never undermined the importance of coming to school, it is significant to delve into the reasons which made them undertake tuition classes. One of the reasons could be lack of academic support from parents. But, they also mentioned lack of exercise or practice questions in the school. Also, the mathematics teacher was teaching through conventional mode of learning. In English classes also, they were just reading the chapter and giving dictation. When it was asked about the chapters they had read, some of the students came up with the name of the chapter as "A Pact with Mr. Smith". All the children in the class could not explain the meaning of the word *"pact"* when asked. They were asked to summarize the story of their choice, which was again a failed endeavor. The researchers tried ways and means so as to put the students under lens of language skills. The students however wanted to learning to be supplemented by the teaching learning materials. They were naming some of the foreign visitors who had taught them using TLMs. The time table on the wall was example of mundane routine of the class 6 students. Their day starts with mathematics period and this is followed for the entire week. So is the case with rest of the subjects. The last period is Homework period which is under supervision of the class teacher. How far the students complete their homework under class teacher's supervision remains a mystery.

## Innovative Practices

Coming from a marginalized section of society, these children do not get any help from home, with their studies. The teachers work very hard to make them learn as much as possible in school. They use creative Teaching Learning Methodologies (TLMs) such as charts, cue cards etc. to make learning fun filled. Some of the TLMs used are the ones developed under the Reach India programme, another significant and successful project of Deepalaya.

*Picture 7.1*

In one of the classes, the class teacher of grade 3 was teaching the students how to see the time on a clock. She even differentiated between the wall clock and wrist watch. The students were responding to her questions, but in Hindi. The teacher used TLM, which was a wooden

*Picture 7.2*

clock which had blocks (See pictures, 7.1 & 7.2). The teachers divided the class into two groups and asked the group to arrange the blocks in same manner as in the clock. She then asked them to rotate the needles of the clock as per the instruction like quarter past six was told to one group of students and quarter past eleven to another group. The children were able to correctly place the needles. Also, the teacher asked to spell the word 'quarter'. Some of the students were able to spell it while others could not. However, the clock activity sets an example of *activity-based learning*. The students were working in a *collaborative* and *cooperative* manner.

The teacher mostly uses materials that are familiar to the students. Like in one of the mathematics class, the teacher used a *dupatta for teaching the shapes and angles. For teaching the difference between the wild and pet animals, the teacher asked about the animals they have seen in the vicinity. The students responded correctly to the pet animals because of their locality they have seen animals such as goat, dogs, cows and buffaloes.*

The teachers use *marbles which are locally available*, plastic toys (animals) which hardly cost ₹ 2, for explaining modes of transportation, they use toys which comes in the packet of some eatable.

### Channelizing the Creativity of Students Through Other Set of Innovative Practices

Combining practical training with theoretical learning to assist teaching, children are taken to various educational trips and parks to learn about environment and historical sites to improve their understanding of our culture and heritage. They have already been taken for picnics to Dolls Musuem, Qutab Minar, Children's Park in Delhi, Taj Mahal in Agra. More such educational trips are being planned. The school promotes latent talent development of children through extracurricular activities that include sports, debates, art and craft, music, dance, drama and painting.

### Social Context of the Slum Learners

The average monthly income of the families of slum learners range from ₹ 1,500 to ₹ 2,500. Also, on an average each family consists of 4 or 5 children apart from their parents. Also, there is system of joint family in most of the clusters. The low levels of income, acts as a deterrent in sending children to school, for many parents. Most of the parents themselves are illiterate, while some are educated till second or fifth standard in their villages. Evidently they did not feel the need to educate their children. Amidst this family situation which includes large family size, low family income and low literacy level of the parents, it is challenging to keep the spirit of educating their children alive for longer time. There is a need to promote awareness among the parents, literate or illiterate to send their wards to the school.

The profession of the parents vary from being domestic servant, factory worker, mason, petty shop owner etc. some of them are even unemployed. The women, mostly illiterate are housewives. Some of them support family income by working in the factories or doing bead work and embroidery or working as domestic helps.

Majority of the people living in Gole Kuan are emigrants who have come from various parts of North India in search of livelihood. Working as labourers or farmers, extreme poverty in their native villages in Bihar, Rajasthan and places as far as Nepal have pushed them to cities like Delhi in search of an occupation. Each community lives in clusters within the Gole Kuan slum. These clusters are referred to by the ethnic groups they represent such as Muslim Basti, Nepali Basti, Balmiki Basti, Bhojpuri Basti and Rajasthani Basti. A population of about 10, 000 in around 3,500 houses in the slum, they celebrate their own festivals and live in harmony with each other. Since the slum dwellers are migrants, the families often move to their native place during the academic session of their wards which jeopardizes the whole education of the learners.

One of the reasons of the formal school education programme is to promote and provide quality education at an affordable cost to children and communities who are socially and economically deprived. The fee for girls is ₹ 100 and for boys ₹ 200.

### The Linkages between School and Community in Educating the Slum Children

Majority of the people living in Gole Kaun are migrants who have come from various parts of North India in search of livelihood. Each community lives in clusters within the Gole kuan slum. During early days Deepalaya faced stiff resistance from some members of the community in setting up the school. There was no existing structure within the slum that could be used as a school. It was with the support of the community that in 1999, a one room structure was built for running the school. Later the community donated some more rooms for the school. The formal school is now spread over ten small, fragmented and vacant building structures within the community.

Since the school is amid the community, there is both advantage and disadvantage to this. It is because the school is amid the community that the people are aware of the various activities that the school promotes and consequently realize the importance of sending their wards to school. The people are often encouraged to see the school children participating in various activities like sports, campaigns, rallies etc. As there is no playground in the school, teachers and volunteers take the students to the nearby playground (MCD playground situated at a distance of 700mts). Also, the morning assembly is held outside the building. This reinforces the community people. It acts as one of the ways to sensitize about the importance of schooling their children.

On one of the days of visit, there was a marriage celebration going on in the morning. Such events are deterrent to the teachers who are burdened with additional responsibility to overcome such events. As it is the school is grappling with the space crunch. The classrooms are very small and they are adjacent to each other, divided via bamboo sheet. The teacher has to overcome the problem of noise and disturbance which she experiences while teaching the students. Also, the houses are constructed in congested manner. The learners can peep outside the windows and can easily be distracted if there is any activity outside the school premises. The community has to compliment the school so as to achieve the goal of educating slum children.

The school conducts parent teacher meetings regularly every month which is well attended by about 90 per cent of the parents. During these meetings, the progress of the children, are discussed with the parents with a view to enhance their academic performance. Apart from these meetings the teachers make regular house visits and also meet parents at school for any special needs of the child.

### Administration and Management

Like any other school administration, this school has a head or principal who looks after the efficient and effective working of the school. This school has an academic staff of 15 teachers including the Principal. There are two male teachers in the school. The non-teaching staff includes two persons (1 aaya and 1 cleaner). The designation of the teaching staff is teachers, there is no grade allocated to them. However, the staff salary is credited in their accounts. The teachers get consolidated salaries. PF is also deducted from the teacher's salary. This clearly shows that the organization caters well to the staff benefits and welfare. Teachers' skills are improved regularly as Deepalaya sends them for various teacher training programmes. However, communication across the organization seems effective. The teachers are accountable for the classroom activities and a weekly report is prepared and collated by the school that is send to the supervisor of Kalkaji school branch where the report is thoroughly checked and feedback is given immediately.

It is interesting to note that the salary of the teachers vary with experience and qualification. There are few teachers who have the basic qualification of being a teacher. They have only attended the training workshops organized by Deepalaya. The range of teachers' salary varies from ₹ 6590 to ₹ 13,025. The sweeper and the music teacher get a consolidated salary of ₹ 5000.

On the basis of interview with the teacher and observation, it can be said that some teachers showed willingness to change to a better school mainly because of low pay scale despite fulfilling qualification. In one of the studies by R. Govinda and N.V. Varghese on social characteristics of teachers in Madhya Pradesh (1993), it was found that some of the teachers in the schools were not because of choice but out of no choice. This is applicable even today when teachers enter the profession without proper degree because she/he has no choice. There is job dissatisfaction among some teachers. They aspire to teach in a better environment. Since this school is scattered in two buildings, the female teachers have to cross a narrow lane while reporting to the main building. The security and safety of the female teachers remain a pertinent issue. Some of the teachers who didn't qualify with the norm showed different teaching style (chalk and talk) as compared to those who are qualified teachers. Some of the teachers were enthusiastically participating in varied teaching activities.

It can be said that while looking for quality education, the socio-economic strata of the teachers should not be sidelined. Job satisfaction among teachers is a significant component for effective learning. The motivation level of the teachers should be increased well in time. It may happen that the teachers working in such difficult situation face the brunt of low motivation level owing to the environment and low pay scale. Each day is challenging for teachers particularly in slums.

Another feature of teaching staff is compulsory House Visits. Persistent advocacy measures, through house to house visits acts as an additional responsibility for the teachers. If the parents fail to report for the PTA, the teachers themselves visit the house to discuss about the performance and development of the learners.

### Intervention of School

On the basis of interaction with the teachers, it was found that the house visits brought a significant change in the life of a slum child.

Mohammed Alam, a 12-year old boy of Gole Kuan slum, wasn't studying anywhere. His father Mr. Mohammed Saddeem and mother Ms. Tanuja Khatoon weren't keen on their children's studies due to extreme poverty. It was found that Alam was studying in his village in Bihar before the family migrated to Delhi but he was diverted from education to earn a livelihood. After many visits and interactions his parents finally agreed to send him to the centre. He stopped coming to school after some time - the reason being his return to the native village (as told by his parents). One of the teachers verified the situation and was shocked to find Alam working in a nearby cycle repair shop. Deepalaya staff met the shopkeeper and explained to him that he was promoting child labour and he could be punished for it. At the same time, parents were also counselled. As a result, Alam came back to the centre and is now a regular student of the school.

Similarly, other alumni of the school braved against all the odds and have set an example for other students studying in the school.

Shabnoor Kadri stays along with her family at Gole Kuan. Her family had migrated to Delhi from Madhya Pradesh a decade ago. She has five sisters among whom Shabnoor is the fifth one. Three of her sisters are married off. Her father and mother are involved with an outsourcing job from an export house. The total annual income of the family is ₹ 10, 000.Shabnoor's childhood was happy and normal like any other child. But, due to an accident at the age of 10 years, her life was shattered forever. Her right leg became permanently disabled and she became dependant on callipers for her movements. The brave girl didn't give up and continued her studies after some time. She completed her secondary education with second division from GTV Inter College, Jhansi. Presently, she is pursuing her higher secondary education in arts stream. She took admission in the IOCL computer centre in May 2010. She was very attentive in the classes and put all her efforts to earn the new skills. She did well in all the evaluation tests conducted in the class. She was also active in other extracurricular activities organized through the centre. After completing the basic computer course, she appeared for the examination of certification conducted by JSS. She secured 'A' grade in the examination. Currently, she is undergoing the advance computer training. Recently, she also got a job as a lab instructor with a computer training institute. Shabnoor is an example for others on how perseverance and hard work can translate hurdles in life into stepping stones of success.

### Challenges

- Drop outs - One of the challenges that the school faces is high dropout rates among students. This is because most of the students are migrants who go back to their villages during harvest season. Many do not return to the slum. Some return after a long gap and that leads to some of the children losing a year or more of studies. Deepalaya however does its best in motivating the parents to continue the studies of their children.
- Expenses—The annual educational expenses for a child are relatively high. Some of the children in this school are sponsored by corporates or individuals. However the

sponsorship amount merely supports the child's education. The remaining money is being given by Deepalaya. Deepalaya encourages parents to pay at least a minimal fee for their wards so that they learn to appreciate and care for their child's education. The fees include expenses incurred on a child's health check-ups as well.

- The major drawback of the school is paucity of space. Any physical activity is dependent on class teacher's efforts to arrange the desks in order to play the activity. The arrangement of the desks is also in a congested fashion leaving it really difficult to take rounds and supervise each child.
- Job satisfaction of teachers-improved pay scale should be given to them.

## Conclusion

Nearly a century ago famous English novelist Charles Dickens began A Tale of Two Cities with the words: "It was the best of times, it was the worst of times, it was the age of wisdom, it was the age of foolishness, it was the epoch of belief, it was the epoch of incredulity, it was the season of Light, it was the season of Darkness, it was the spring of hope, it was the winter of despair, we had everything before us, we had nothing before us…" Today more people have more money than ever before. Yet we have more poverty than ever before in certain isolated rural communities and in the slum areas of metropolis. Almost everywhere one can find comfortable affluence side by side with deprivation and poverty. There are more high school graduates than ever before; there are also more dropouts. There is more education; there is no education also, in particular to poor, deprived children living in slums. There is more success at the policy making than ever before in the form of rights like RTE 2009 and also more failure when it comes to implementation of the same right. "It is the best of times; it is the worst of times." A survey of slum dwellings in Delhi brings out a very interesting and important social, economic and educational intricacy surrounding the slum children per se. There are still unanswered questions which arises when one scrutinize the existence or mere mention of Directive Principles in Article 45 of the Indian Constitution which prescribes that the state shall endeavor to provide, within a period of ten years from the commencement of the Constitution, for free and compulsory education for all children until they reach the age of 14 or latest right being Right to free and Compulsory Education, 2009. By what time these rights will be effective and meaningful to the poor and deprived children of our society poses a greatest challenge before us.

## REFERENCES

Chauhan, C. (2009). No school for slum children in India's capital. *Hindustan Times*. 15 January 2009.

Gore, M.S. (2000): *Third Survey of Research in Sociology and Social Anthropology*, Vol.1, Manak Publication.

Kaul, R. (2001). Accessing Primary education: Going beyond the Classroom. *Economic and Political Weekly*, Vol. 36, No. 2, pp.155-162.

Kumar, N. and Aggrawal, S. C. (2003). Patterns of consumption and Poverty in Delhi Slums. *Economic and Political Weekly*, Vol. 38, No. 50, pp-5294-5300.

Sudarshan, Ratna M. (2000): 'Educational Status of Girls and Women: The Emerging Scenario' in Rekha Wazir (ed), *The Gender Gap in Basic Education: NGOs as Change Agents*. New Delhi: Sage Publications.

Tsujita, Yuko. (2009). Deprivation of Education in urban Areas: A basic Profile of Slum Children in Delhi, India. Institute of Developing Economies (IDE), Jetro, Japan

# 8

# Child Schooling in India

## *The North-East India Perspectives*

***Rupashree Paul and Bornita Purkayastha***

Education is the basic requirement for human development. Therefore, the child schooling has far reaching influence on shaping the living styles of the human beings, in particular, and social and economic development of the society in general. Typically, child schooling is provided in schools, where the child stage in steadily advancing classes until she/he completes it and moves on to the higher level of education. The major goals of child schooling are achieving basic literacy and innumeracy amongst all pupils, as well as establishing in them the foundations in science, mathematics, geography, history and other social sciences. A large body of evidence suggests that workers productivity and earnings depends not only on years of education acquired but also on what is learnt at school. The general economic model shows that child schooling is determined by gender, age of the child, relationship of the child to the to the household head, gender of household, education status of household head, regional differences and access to school. In this paper we have re-examined these issues in the process of child schooling. The child schooling creates the base for the holistic developments of the individuals of a country as well as the total development of the country itself in many ways.

### Child Schooling Age

The age between six to twelve years is the most important stage of child, where he goes through many important physical, psychological, and social changes. At this stage, the real being of the child is being formulated, shaped and reshaped. During this stage child involves himself/herself in many creative and developmental activities for his/her overall development. Child entry in the school gives the child a very different experience which is totally different from the home atmosphere. In this phase of life the child passes through many stages of inter and intra conflicts which reinforce the child's moral will to become a good future citizen. More or less children usually have smooth and strong motor skills in this stage. Child development at schooling age describes the development of the expected physical, emotional and mental abilities of children of 6-14 years age. Lying, cheating, stealing, playing, enjoying, joking etc. are all examples of behaviours that school age children perform. During this stage, they learn how to negotiate the expectations and rules placed on them by family, friends, school and society. A six years old child should be able to focus on a task for at least 15 minutes. By age nine, a child should be able to focus attention for about an hour. When children reach school age years they are eager learners, naturally imaginative and creative. Moreover, school age children learn by doing as they interact with their peers and explore the materials in their environment. U.S. National Library of Medicine (National Institutes of Health) points out some safety measures for school age children as follows.

- School age children are highly active. They need physical activity and peer approval and want to try more doing and adventures behaviour.
- Swimming and water safety lessons may help prevent drawing.
- Safety instruction regarding matches, lighters, barbecues, stoves and open fires can prevent major burns.
- Wearing seat belts is the most important wary to prevent major injury or death from a motor vehicle accident.
- Children should be target to play sports in appropriate safe, supervised areas, with proper equipment and rules. Bicycles, Skateboards, in-line skates and other types of recreational sports equipment should fir the child.

## Child Schooling in India

In 1950, India made a constitutional commitment to provide free and compulsory education to all chiidren up to the age of 14. In 2002, a constitutional amendment made free and compulsory education a fundamental right for children aged 6-14. Over the past two decades demand for schooling in India has increased, but provision is unequal. The National Policy on Education (NPE, 1986) and its programme of Action (POA, 1992) state that all children, irrespective of caste, creed, location or gender, should have access to elementary education of a comparable quality, but in reality, schooling provision favours those better off, and disadvantaged groups (including poor children, girls, children from Scheduled caste (SC), Scheduled Tribe (ST), Other Backward Classes (OBC)) groups have less access and access to poorer quality education.

National Policy on Education (NPE, 1986) focused on the need for improvements to school environments (including building conditions, availability of tap water and toilet facilities), instructional materials and teacher and teacher training. The District Primary Education Programme (1994) brought additional resources to the sector through the involvement of bilateral and multilateral donors. Village education committees, parent teacher and mother–teacher association have become active across the country. Despite of these changes, quality of provision continues to be a concern and is highlighted in the tenth (2002-2007) and Eleventh (2007-2012) five year plans as well as SSA (Sarva Siksha Abhiyan). National Programme for Education of Girls at Elementary Level (NPEGL) and Kasturba Gandhi Balika Vidyalaya (KGBV) target girls often from scheduled castes, scheduled tribes and minorities in difficult areas. Through these programmes, scholarships, free uniforms and textbooks are being given to recipients. The Mid-day Meal scheme offers free lunch to all children attending primary schools throughout India.

Provision of quality education in India is an enormous quantitative challenge. The number of primary school has grown rapidly from 529,000 in 1986 to 767,000 in 2005 and at upper primary schools from 134,000 to 275,000 (CREATE, 2009). In 2003, around 87 per cent of habitation had a primary school within a distance of 1 km and 78 per cent of habitations had an upper primary school within 3 km (NCERT, 2005). In 2004-2005, data available from the Ministry of Human Resource development (MHRD) showed that 182 million students were enrolled in 1.04 million elementary schools (grade 1-8) across the country (GoI, 2007a). In 2004-2005 around 88 per cent of boys and 79 per cent of girls were attending schools nationally (GoI, 2007b). According to the census report 2011, the national literacy rate is 74.04 per cent (82.14 per cent male literacy and 65.46 per cent female literacy). The gender difference in child schooling is one of the most fundamental problems found in India. Drez and Kingdon (2001) have found strong evidence of sharp gender bias in school participation in rural north India states of Uttar Pradesh, Bihar, Madhya Pradesh and Rajasthan. Later in rural west Bengal in Eastern India, Pal (2004) found that mother's literacy significantly enhances the probability of school enrolment among girls but it is insignificant for boys. Similarly father's education significantly encourages boys schooling only and does not have any perceptible impact on girls. Education of tribal children is another issue in India. There are 753 Scheduled Tribes living in different parts of the country. According to the 2001 census, the tribal child population in India is 74.6 million. The largest number of tribes is in undivided Madhaya Pradesh (16.40 million), followed by Odisha (7 million) and Jharkand (6.6 million). Education of ST Children is considered important, not only because of the constitutional obligation but also because of the input for total development of tribal communities. There were 16 million ST Children (10.87 years) as of March 2001; out of the total child population in India of about 193 million in the age group of 6-14 years (SES, 2001) Government of India). ST Children face problems wherever teachers don't speak their dialects at all. From the perspective of language, it is desirable to have a local teacher from the same tribal community (Jha & Jhingran, 2002). The evidences suggest that tribal children do possess the basic cognitive abilities and psychological dispositions necessary for successful participation in school. Yet tribal children have very low levels of participation and success in school education programmes. Beside these, other fundamental problems in child schooling in India are malnutrition, wastage and stagnation, illness, poverty, child labour etc.

### Child Schooling in North East India

North East India is educationally one of the least developed regions of India. The literacy rate of the region was 55.63 per cent which is very less than the national average 63.37 per cent in 2001. They are the first generation learners and this region is educationally underdeveloped like anything.

Education is one of the principal factors influencing the quality of the country's labour force. It has an important role in the socio-economic

**Table 8.1 : State-wise number of Recognized Primary and Middle Schools (2005-06 to 2007-08)**

| States | *2005-06* | | *2006-07* | | *2007-08* | |
|---|---|---|---|---|---|---|
| | *Primary/ Junior Basic* | *Middle/ Senior Basic Schools* | *Primary/ Junior Basic* | *Middle/ Senior Basic Schools* | *Primary/ Junior Basic* | *Middle/ Senior Basic Schools* |
| Arunachal Pradesh | 1380 | 528 | 1438 | 588 | 1561 | 664 |
| Assam | 30499 | 9716 | 30094 | 11347 | 30094 | 11347 |
| Manipur | 2552 | 831 | 2563 | 769 | 2563 | 769 |
| Meghalaya | 5851 | 1759 | 6351 | 2259 | 6618 | 2259 |
| Mizoram | 1688 | 1121 | 1700 | 1081 | 1700 | 1081 |
| Nagaland | 1520 | 481 | 1520 | 481 | 1662 | 465 |
| Sikkim | 733 | 205 | 761 | 217 | 772 | 221 |
| Tripura | 1863 | 1004 | 1998 | 1007 | 2151 | 1021 |

*Source*: Ministry of Human Resource development, Govt of India.

development in North East India. Its contribution to economic growth and its impact on population controls, life expectancy, and infant mortality, improving nutritional status and strengthening civil institutions is well recognized in North East India. As per National Policy on Education (1986), priority has been accorded to the universalisation of primary education for children in the age group of 6 to 14 years. There has been a great deal of accomplishment in the field of education since 1950-51.The following tables show that state wise number of recognized primary / Junior basic and middle / senior basic school in North East India (2005-06 to 2007-08) and management wise number of High / Post basic schools NER, (2006-2007).

**Table 8.2: State/Management-wise Number of High Schools in NER, (2006-07)**

| *State* | *Govt* | | *Local Bodies* | | *Private Aided* | | *Private Unaided* | | *Total* |
|---|---|---|---|---|---|---|---|---|---|
| | *Number* | *Percentage per cent* | *Number* | *Percentage per cent* | *Number* | *Percentage per cent* | *Number* | *Percentage per cent* | |
| Arunachal Pradesh | 109 | 73.15 | 0 | 0 | 17 | 11.41 | 23 | 15.44 | 149 |
| Assam | 2793 | 55.29 | 0 | 0 | 935 | 18.51 | 1324 | 26.21 | 5052 |
| Manipur | 201 | 28.67 | 0 | 0 | 102 | 14.55 | 398 | 56.18 | 701 |
| Meghalaya | 14 | 2.07 | 0 | 0 | 458 | 67.75 | 204 | 30.18 | 676 |
| Mizoram | 191 | 38.12 | 0 | 0 | 126 | 25.15 | 184 | 36.67 | 501 |
| Nagaland | 125 | 31.41 | 0 | 0 | 273 | 68.59 | 0 | 0 | 398 |
| Sikkim | 95 | 84.82 | 0 | 0 | 1 | 0.89 | 16 | 14.29 | 112 |
| Tripura | 395 | 93.16 | 1 | 0.24 | 9 | 2.12 | 19 | 4.48 | 424 |

*Source*: Minister of Human Resource Development, Govt. of India

## Problems of Child Schooling: A North East Indian Perspective

Article 45 of our constitution ensures free and compulsory primary education for every child up to age of 14 years. But it has not been able to fulfil the task till today due to various issues specially found in North East India. Theoretical literature on child labour has stressed the role of poverty as one of the main determinant of parent's decision to send their children to work rather than to school in North East region. Impulse NGO Networking Shillong, Meghalaya (2004) found that 71 per cent children in the sample are literate whereas 29 per cent children are illiterate. These children work 8-12 hours a day and on an average earn ₹ 10-50 per day.

These children give up their studies due to family problems to give financial support to their families and some children do not have interest in studies. One of the important problems of language is found in Assam. The language problem is faced by the tribal children in Assam whose home language is different from the regional language, which is the medium of instruction at the primary level. Another important problem is gender-biasness. Girls are more likely than boys to be not attending schools in North East India. Gender disparities in enrolments have reduced, especially in richer states, but girls remain more likely to drop out where enrolment rates are low. Boys often withdraw from school for economic reasons, while girls are more likely to be involved in domestic chores. Children from households with little or no previous educational experience are more likely to be excluded from schooling. Malnutrition and repeated illness combined with a lack of healthcare facilities lead many children to drop out or not attending school. Despite of the implementation of Operation Backboard schemes in the country in the late 1980s, north eastern states still have single teacher primary schools. The education system is not very efficient as because the schools function for relatively less number of days and the dropout rate is relatively high. Beside these, some of the other issues are pinpointed as follows:

- Over Population,
- Costly Programme,
- Single point entry and Institutional system of Education,
- Inadequate programmes of spreading literacy,
- Lack of exercise of compulsion,
- Poverty,
- Prejudges against education of girls.
- Dull Curriculum,
- Lack of adequate proper equipment.
- Poor administration,
- Lack of Trained teachers and single teacher school.

## Suggestive Measures for overcoming the Obstacles of Child Schooling in North East India

The tenth five year plan (2002-2007) has emphasized on the matter that all children in the 6-14 age group should have access to primary schools, upper primary schools or their alternatives within a walking distance of one km and three km respectively. Eleventh five year plan (2007-2012) also had more targets in the elementary education in North East India. Sarva Shiksha Abhiyan (SSA) is a flagship programme of government of India to support the states in creating, developing and strengthening the formal primary and upper primary school system to achieve the goals of UEE. If we want our primary education system to serve the quality education, we must mobilize the creative talent of the vast human resources which is lying as stagnant condition. This is the need of the day, only when the quality of teaching is good, primary education can successfully meet the dilemmas of quantity vs. quality, accountability vs. autonomy, creativity vs. convergence and equity vs. excellence. Teachers are considered to be the most important component of the child schooling. Hence, supporting for their development is very crucial and necessary for the success of the primary education system. All schools should have buildings, toilets, drinking water, electricity, playgrounds, blackboards and other facilities. There must be provision of one classroom for every teacher at the elementary stage. Some valuable measures or suggestions have to be taken to overcome these issues relating to child schooling in North East India. These are as:

- Multiple entries into the schooling system in this region.
- Part time classes should be managed for the children as they are involved in household activities.
- Sub school scheme should be arranged with low population.
- The task should be the teaching of the 3R's good manners, healthy habits, some life oriented skills with hand general knowledge etc. ··
- Improving the building and equipment
- More number of teachers should be employed in each school.
- Reform the educational administration.

## Conclusion

The child schooling in North East India presents a broad spectrum with gender biases leading to poor education and health of children and development constraints. However, in order to realize the full potentials of child schooling, the government needs to play a more active role in promoting and supporting the child schooling in the rural areas of North East India. The parents and teachers should properly handle the development process of the children. Government and non-governmental organizations should adopt some remedial measures for the improving conditions of Child schooling in North East India.

## REFERENCE

Directorate of Census (2011). Provisional Census Data Government of India : New Delhi.

Government of India (2001). National Human Development Report, 2001. Websit (Access on 24 August 2011).

Government of India (2007a). *Selected Educational Statistics, 2004-2005*. New Delhi: Ministry of Human Resource Development.

Government of India (2007b). *Annual Report, 2006-2007*. New Delhi: Ministry of Human Resource Development.

Dreze, Jean and Gita G. Kingdon (2001). School Participation I Rural India, *Review of* Development Economics, 5 (1), PP1-24.

Kambhampati, U.S. and Pal, Sarmistha (2001). Role of Parental literacy in Explaining Gender Difference: Evidence from Child Schooling in India. *The European Journal of Developmental Research*, 13 (2) PP. 97-11

Pal, Sarmistha. (2004). How much of the gender difference in child school enrolment can be explained? Evidence from rural India. *Bulletine of Economic Research, 56, 0305*-3378, pp.133-158.

The Report of Sarva Shiksha Abhiyan, Delhi (2009). Retrived on 31st October 2011 from http:// www.edudel.nic.in/ssa/brouchure/ss.pdf.

# 9

# Female Dropouts in Primary Education

## *A Case Study on Santhals of Odisha*

*Sipra Sagarika*

Education has been in consideration as the cardinal aspect of socio-economic development, both at micro and macro levels since long past. But more specifically modern education has proved itself to have greater implications on sharing up of the overall development goals at the levels of individuals, families, communities, and finally nation as a whole. Socio-economically a nation is more advanced if the people are literate and that is where education comes to the spotlight. This universal truth has made many developing and developed countries work and formulate policies for compulsory education. And out of the several phases of the educational process, the primary education is the basic foundation to all other stages of education. In rural and interior settings of the geographical contours the worst affected portion is primary education. It shapes the productivity of the state and individual. In total education improves the self esteem, empowerment of people, and preserves the democratic notions of functioning. In case of India almost all major states such as Kerala, Uttar Pradesh, Madhya Pradesh, Maharashtra, Odisha, Bihar, and West Bengal etc are therefore trying their best to improve the quality of basic education. It is, therefore in this context that not only the social scientists but also the economists have started to concentrate on the research and analysis aspect of the relevance of education for all through different phases. For instance Education as explained by Durkheim aims towards transmission of norms and values. The survival of the society in a collective form is possible mainly because of sufficient form of homogeneity among various members of the society. Education preserves and reinforces these homogenizing principles of society in a child from the beginning. Durkheim (1956:17) writes, "Education is the influence exercised by the adult generation on those that are not yet ready for social life. Its object is to arouse and to develop in the child a certain number of physical, intellectual, and moral states which are demanded of him by political society as a whole and social milieu for which he is specially destined". Education is another key stone to demarcate the human development index and the most essential aspect to note here is that literacy and spread of education among women. It has tremendous impact on the lifestyle and the achievement capabilities, reproductive and health behaviours (UNESCO report 2006:141). Therefore, one of the key elements of study in the paper is gender. Further each state runs with its socio- cultural patterns of distribution of population, and Odisha is predominantly marked with various' jatis 'and' prajatis' of tribal people. Thus it is essential to understand the currents of educational patterns among the tribal people of Odisha and primarily status of female tribal education in the context of primary schooling.

Tribal education acts as an agent of transmission of culture from one generation to another and brings several socio-economic transformations in the traditional society. Education is also a powerful instrument of social change and also reshapes the personality of the individual. As per 2001 census the number of scheduled Tribe female literates is 2, 95, and 832. The highest of which is at Sundargarh with 79, 842 while Cuttack has lowest 4, 872 in the State. Odisha occupies a prominent space in the tribal map of India for two reasons, first concentration of tribal population is much higher than any other state, and secondly there is presence of large varieties of tribal communities. There are 62 types of tribal communities found in Odisha. Size of the tribal population of Odisha varies from a few persons among the Chenchu to about ten Lakh among the Kondh. Some of the tribe like Bhumija, Gond, Kisan, Munda, Kharia, Santhal, and Batudi etc are concentrated in the Northern and Western Odisha. Saura, Knodh, Sabara, Lodha etc are largely confined to the Southern Odisha. According to the 2001 census the total Scheduled tribe population of the State is 8, 145, 081. The tribal population of Odisha constitutes of 8.08 per cent of the total population of the country. Tribal population is highly concentrated in the district like Koraput, Mayurbhanj, Sundargarh, Keonjhar and Phulbani then in the coastal plain consisiting of Balasore, Cuttack, Puri, and Ganjam. It is observed that the percentage of literacy among 42 tribes is below the State average of 14.96 per cent. There are seven tribes among whom the percentage of literacy among the tribal population is far below then five per cent. It is also noticed that the percentage of literacy among the tribal population is far below then the literacy percentage of general population at the district level. Likewise in comparison to male literacy percentage of tribal group, female literacy percentage is much less. For example, according to 2001 census literacy rate of the tribal male of Odisha is three times more than the tribal female literacy.

## Education and Tribal Women

Education among the tribal women is important for two reasons—first, education help them in coming out of the traditional cocoon to create a new community. Secondly, it can help them in widening their outlook, to make them conscious of their rights and status in the society. Educated tribal women can act as the agent of social change in their communities.

Recent scenario of literacy of tribal women in Odisha varies from region to region as well as from tribe to tribe. Not only a wide gap is found between literacy rate of general population and tribal population but a similar gap is found in the literacy rate of tribal male and female.

Santhal as a major tribe occupy a prominent position among the tribes in India. They were distributed in the adjacent States of Odisha such as Bihar, West Bengal, and Assam. They have to live in different social conditions in different geographical locations and different demographic environment to earn their livelihood. It is enthusiastic to know that among the Santhals the extreme cases of both the traditionality and modernity exists in hand in hand.Some of them are living in the accessible hilly tracks while some of them are living in the town areas, and some are highly educated and placed in high posts while some others are illiterates and are unskilled. While some others are highly established political leaders, some from the same community are even ignorant about their political rights. The Santhals are considered to be the most educated and progressive ones as compared to the other communities. They have developed their own language i.e. Santali language and have their own script *Ol Chiki.*

But the paradoxical situation arises when massive female dropouts are marked at level of schooling despite of its progressiveness. The gravity of the situation intensifies with the failure of State Government's initiation to introduce stipends for tribal school children. The large scale dropouts at the primary education subsequently impacts negatively the later literacy rates of the tribal female and de reservation of seats at the University level is marked. Presently Santhal are going through a critical period of transition because old social structural arrangements have been distributed by many socio- economic political and psychological factors. Therefore an attempt to study the deeper reasons behind such problem is relevant.

## Studies on Tribal Schooling Patterns in India

There have been several studies on the patterns of tribal schooling mechanism. The trends and functioning of tribal schools in the tribal belts and rural areas are studied. S.N. Rath (1992: 24) in his study marks that in many cases, existence and functioning of tribal students are found only in records. In reality there are wider spread disparities. Further K. Maulik (1998:72-73) in his work about situation of tribal females in the North Odisha explains that the tribal female members are poor in local dialects or language leading to sever communication gap in the daily activities . Thus, he infers that education would definitely enhance the condition of female in the tribal community and make them competent enough to deal with the outer world. Adding on to this, S. Rout (1985: 64) in his in-depth study on tribal education in 13 districts of Odisha marked that the low scholastic and motivational achievements were marked among female students and major causes of female dropouts in Santhal were socio-economic, psychological in its nature. Further, Binita (1984: 33) identified the problems of education of Santhala as apathy of community members to education, enrolment, and retention, relevance of content education, employment opportunities, alienation and communication. Further, S.L. Mohapatra (1967: 42) in his study explains that education is hardly imparted through their mother tounge. No proper curricular have been framed befitting local culture and tradition. School education does not orient the tribal children towards pursuing of their own mode of life. In phonology and Syntax, the tribal languages are quite different from the medium of instructions like Odia, except in certain mutually borrowed items due to their close contact over a long period of time. This is partly responsible for student dropouts and poor performances in education.

## Methodology

The study is descriptive in nature. It concentrates on describing the evident trends of girl student dropouts in the santal prangans. It is an attempt to trace the situation in their natural setting. The Shyamakhunta block of Mayurbhanj district is the field for study. It is situated within a radius of 8km from the District head quarter Baripada and includes 70 villages. Mayurbhanj District is the highest in total number of tribal population but in case of total literacy rate it gets 15th position in the state. The District of Mauyrbhanj was declared as scheduled area from 26th January 1950. Merger of Mayurbhanj took place on the 1st January 1949. As a result of which it emerged as a district of Odisha. Mayurbhanj district is bounded under North by Midnapur District of West Bengal and Singhbum District of Bihar, on the South Keonjhar and Balasore districts of Odisha, on the West by Singhbum and Keonjhar district in the East in Balasore district in Odisha. The District contains hilly areas which divide it into 4-sub-divisions namely the Central division comprising of the Sadar Baripada, Kaptipada: subdivision, the North Western division comprising of Bamanghati subdivision. And the South Western division comprising the Panchapir subdivision. These three subdivisions have four towns namely Baripada, Rairangpur, Karanjia and Udala. Baripada is the headquarter of the Maurbhanj district. All the registered primary schools under the State are the plot of study.

It is expected that the tribal literacy rate of Mayurbhanj would be higher as compared to other states because of three reasons i.e. First , kings of Mayurbhanj wanted to spread education among the people. Secondly, Christian missionaries also wanted to educate the tribal people. Thirdly, after independence government has taken many steps to educate tribal people. Many ashrams and Kanyashrams are located in Mayurbhanj District and the teachers, school staffs, parents, female dropouts and continuing students of the course comprehended the universe of the study.

There are mainly three reasons behind the choice of the research field (location) as such-First, Mayurbhanj district has the highest concentration of the Santhal population and it is the target community of the study. Therefore demarcation of education trends, in the area can be a fruitful one. Secondly, imprints of urbanization in the Shyamakhunta block are evident due to its clear proximity to the district capital. Therefore an analysis of problem of female dropouts can project the grim reality. Thirdly, the human environment which surrounds these people and the socio-economic structures in which they are living is free from direct influcncc of any big industrial set-up, thus they can be studied in their natural settings.

The tools used for data collection from the field include observation, interview schedule, and case analysis. Further, participatory assessment approach (PAA), focused group discussion (FGDs), and in-depth interviews (IDIs). Even the narratives of the respondents are encouraged. In case use of technological assistance of audio and video recording a series of methodological layers of transcription , coding and data matrices are used to simplify the data collection.

## Tribal Female Dropout in Primary Education—Reasons

Through the process of observation its quite evident that tribal female dropouts in primary education occurs mainly because their parents engage girls in traditional patterns of earning livelihood and confirm to primitive patterns of tribal division of labour. Several interviews with the parents of the dropped out girl students reflected that, there is an imbalance between the needs of education and economic needs of the tribal families which leads to dropouts. For instance while interviewing on the dropout "Maisingi's father "Bikuna Majhi" said that, *when my family is going to sleep in hungry stomach, I need money and Maisingi's domestic work at babu's kotha brings money to get food, can her education instantly do the same for me?"* Through Participatory Assessment Approach (PAA), and Focused Group Discussions (FGDs) with the community members further stratifications were marked in the primary schooling on the basis of gender plots. For instance, it was expressed in the community discussion that a gendered demarcation between Santhal boys and Santhal girl students, always worked as a haltin the tribal female education. It is marked that no impact of the urban setting works, when it comes to female education as there is sever lack of orientation among Saanthal parents and members of the community.

Several constraints can be marked out in relation to women education among the tribal. The methods of recording and decoding of the tribal language could help in deriving such inferences. It is marked that the constraints can be broadly categorized into two types i.e. First she has to face constraint as a member of the tribal society. These constraints can be categorized under "general constraint" as the tribal boys also face the same problems. Secondly, there are "specific constraints" which only the female member of the community faces.

The general constraints are like inadequacy of the sufficient numbers of educational institutions in educating tribal people, the tribal student enrolment as per 2001 census in Klahandi district is considerably low as there are only ten 'seva ashrams' available for tribal education.

Secondly, for the educational development of the tribal areas stringent steps are not taken by the government.

Thirdly, while there was discussion with the teachers functioning in the schools as well, the problems faced from the side of the teachers were uncovered. For instance –

(i) teachers who do not have dedication towards their occupation are getting their appointment in the tribal areas i.e "punitive postings".

(ii) Most of the teachers are non-tribal and they are from the plain areas, so they do not want to stay in the tribal areas as a consequence of which there are "proxy teachers" are found, who teach the students in place of the real ones, thus leading to the deteriorated standard of education.

(iii) In some other cases when the teacher does not get an option of a comfortable stay in the tribal area, they prefer to stay at their own place and commute, this further encourages irregularities and fluctuations in the daily attendance of the teachers presence in the school.

(iv) As most of the teachers do not have a proper knowledge in the tribal language and culture, that creates an obstacle in keeping close contacts with tribal students. Even the teachers cannot create awareness among the tribal people to send their children to the school due to lack of knowledge regarding the tribal language.

(v) Teachers appointed in the tribal areas take full advantage of lack of supervision of higher authority. They only come out to schools as per the schedule on the pay days or in any case of inspections. These worsen the situation and encourage the dropouts.

When in depth interviews were made with the parents of the tribal female students, it was marked that some other specific constraints for the tribal female are –

(i) Parents prefer to send their daughters to the girl school or the 'kanyashrams' and the number of such ashramas in Odisha is limited. This ends up in halting the girls in access of education.

(ii) Tribal parents are reluctant to send their girl child to primary schools where the teacher posted is a gents and in all most all the primary schools the teacher is a male, very rarely one finds instances of female teachers in those interior places.

(iii) As a reflection of the patriarchal society the parents give priority to the son's education even though the girl child is interested in pursuing the education or does better then the son in examination.

(iv) Further, when the female dropout in first hand " Sudha " was asked for the reason of her dropout, she indicated towards the infrastructural problem for the tribal girl child as the un-availability of a safe and hygienic toilet facility, which most of these primary education centres are not looked after with care. This discourages most of the girl children to withhold long hours of classes leading to absenteeism and health problems. Further, Community people along with parents reveal that if their daughter is getting education then they find difficulty in finding a groom for her.

(vi) The tribal girls are very hard working in their nature, they do the entire house work chorus and they also look after the young siblings.

So the parents are relieved with the responsibilities sharing, leading to reluctance behaviour for the school option. Thus, poor economic conditions coupled with several socio-cultural constraints are responsible for the encouragement of the tribal girl child drop outs in the primary education in the district.

**Credentials to the Study**

Several other studies have been also conducted to trace the aetiologies of the tribal female dropouts which coincide with the present study as well. A brief layout of such studies would formulate the plot of pre implications of the research in a better way. Education (Kothari Commission) (1996) points out that drop out among the school children mainly that in 65 per cent of cases, takes place due to poverty of parents. In a later study conducted by NCAER in 1994, it is also pointed out that economic factors are more important than any other factors for this syndrome (Tilak, 2006: 38). Further in the Human Development Report of Odisha–2004, depicts some independent reasons such as financial weakness (15.3 per cent), working as earners of families (14.5 per cent), engagement in household works (12.3 per cent), child not interested to study (10 per cent), problems with teachers (7.2 per cent), difficulties in learning (6.2 per cent), difficulties in reaching school (5.8 per cent), parents not interested in studies (4.5 per cent), migration (0.8 per cent), completion of the desired level (0.5 per cent), sibling care (0.3 per cent).

In another study conducted by A.B Ota and R.P.Mohanty in the tribal concentration regions of Mayurbhanj district, it is similarly explained that dropout takes place due to the amalgamation of multiple factors and major among them is the cultural stigmas of negative notions attached to the education of tribal females by the community and the parents themselves.

### Implications of the Research

The identification of the reasons behind the female dropouts in the primary education of Santhal community, would complement to the provison of Article 46 of the Constitution of India which provides the promotion of the educational interest of Scheduled tribe and Scheduled caste people and for their protection against social injustice and exploitation. The New Education Policy, 1986 aimed at creating an environment focusing on tribal child education along with emphasis on vanovidyalays and sisu seva-ashrams. But, still the grim condition of the tribal children continued, clearly indicating the failures at the implementation level. Thus, the outcomes of the research can further add government in framing its policies in a practical manner leading to its proper execution. Further the introduction of the 'Mid-Day Meal' scheme even could not prove its purpose to attract parents to send their children to the schools due to the massive corruption at the level of administration, and execution.

Amidst all such gloomy realities, there still exists an optimistic hope that the educational system should be built up in an all inclusive manner. In this context an attempt to build up a meaningful educational system as explained by Coomarswamy is appreciable and practicable. This can also be interpreted as a suggestive measure to reduce the tribal female drop outs in the primary education system. According to him an ideal educational system which would reduce all malice and should have

(i) universal philosophical attitude, (ii) recognition of the sacred and the profane elements of the education system, (iii) to develop etiquette-civilization conceived as the product of the civil people, (iv) improvised relationship between students and teachers, (v) altruism and recognition of unity of life, (vi) control of thoughts and action all together through education. This can definitely alter the gloomy state of tribal female dropout.

## Conclusion

This paper deals with identification of the causes leading to tribal female child dropouts in the primary education in Santhal community, in the Mauyrbhanj district of Odisha. It also makes an attempt to evaluate a part of the Government projects and policies in addressing the problems of the tribal education. In order to retain the progressive status of the Santhal community, checks on such specific malaise in the primary education must be implemented. With the identification of such problems, ideas such as "*learning and earning*" may help in curtailing the girl child drop outs in primary education. A comprehensive strategy to fight out the problem of tribal female dropouts needs to be developed. A combined strategic empowerment of both tribal girl and tribal women empowerment can act as a catalyst. The non-governmental organization (NGOs) should be made agent of capacity builder for tribal families and should build up awareness and motivation to tribal parents to allow their girl children to be educated properly. Further the identified problems of the drop outs can be addressed through the right implications and the recommendations of the Dhebar Commission Report of 1961, by the Government of India. As per the commission the teacher should take interest not only in the enrolment of the students to the school but also in the regular attendance. They can do this by visiting the houses of the absentee students to encourage them to attend school and to strengthen the rapport between the teacher taught and the parents. Teachers who do such jobs would appropriately reward in the form of extra allowance and the students who are regular to schools should be encouraged by proper incentives like prizes and gifts. Along with these steps, the institutional building of "tribal education" can be framed. Further it requires the popular participation of the whole community and the related agents as well. With such steps perhaps the challenges of the wide female dropouts in the primary education in the Santhal community can be checked and status of the Santhal women literacy can be enhanced.

## REFERENCES

Apte, Dalf, (1997). Educational Change, Akhil Bharatiya Vidyarthi Parishad, New Delhi.

Agragami. (1994). "Adivasi Anchalara Samastanka Paien Sikhya" (odiya). Raigada: Education Department, Agragami, Kashipur.

Behura. N.K. (1990). "Constarints in Tribal Culture for Formal Education" in B. Chaudhary (ed) *Education and Literacy Programme*. New Delhi: Inter-India Publication.

Bhowmik, K.L. (1971). "Tribal India, a profile in Indian ethnology" The World Press Private Ltd. Kolkata.

Bose, M.K. (1971) *Tribal Life in India*. New Delhi: National Book Trust of India.

Chottapadhyay, K.P. (1973). Education, The tribal people of India. New Delhi: Government of India Publication.

Elwin Verrier (ed). (1963). A New Deal for Tribal India. Ministry of Home Affairs Government of India, New Delhi.

Dube,.S.C. (1960). "Approaches to the Tribal Problems" in L.P, Vidyarthi (ed.) *Indian Anthropology in Action* .Council of Social and Cultural Research, Ranchi, Bihar.

Government of India Report (1961). Report Commission for Scheduled Areas and Scheduled Tribes, New Delhi: Manager of Publication, New Delhi.

Mohapatra, L.K. (1967), "Curricular, Methods and Text Books in Tribal Education", Report on Tribal Education in India, N.C.E.R.T, New Delhi.

Pasayat, C. (1993). "Literacy in Odisha", *Odisha Review*, XLIX (09): 42-43, New Delhi.

Pasayat, C. (1994) "The State of Female Literacy among Tribal people of Odisha," *Odisha Review* LI (3): 4-8.

Rath, S.N. (1992). "Literacy in Tribal India: An Evaluation" in B. Chaudhari (ed), *Education and Literacy Programmes*. New Delhi.

Viswas, P.C. (1954). Santals of Santal Pranganas, Bharatiya Adina Jatisangha, New Delhi.

# 10

# Schools as Spaces for Addressing Child Sexual Abuse

*Vertika Chowdhary*

"My uncle thinks I'm cute, so he likes playing with me. But I don't like the way he hugs and kisses me. He makes me do things and says this is our little secret. I don't know what to do. I'm scared to tell mummy because she likes my uncle and won't believe me."

*Innocence Violated*, India Today Article, 2002

"Sexual abuse of children in any form by a family member is among the most urgent forms of child abuse which our society must address. A report produced by the BBC opined that close-knit family life in India masks an alarming amount of sexual abuse."

*Incest, Child Abuse is India's Hidden Shame*, Merinews Article, 2009

Wives who make allegations of sexual abuse of their children by their husbands suffer from "some peculiar psychiatric condition". The alleged sexual abuse of an "infant child (who would have just passed her suckling stage then)" is a "seemingly incredulous" accusation to make. An allegation of child sexual abuse by a mother will be "concocted to wreak her vengeance" on her husband.

The medical examinations carried out at the behest of a mother which reveal "a wide vaginal opening—wider than would be expected of their age group" will at most support the probability of "what a mother might do with the little female child for creating evidence of sex abuse".

*"A father is a father...and even if he is a bad father he still has the right to his children..."*

(Supreme Court, in Satish Mehra vs Delhi administration)

*To Think the Unthinkable*, Outlook Magazine, 1997

The above excerpts, taken from various magazines, aptly capture both, the veracity of child sexual abuse as well as social unwillingness to accept it as a reality, in India. Articles on child sexual abuse, and many contemporary films in Indian cinema like *Monsoon Wedding, Traffic Signal, and Page3* etc., highlight its contours and map its prevalence. Many of them bring out that home and particularly joint families are very vulnerable contexts. They also point out the fact that prevalence is very high among the urban elite. There is a higher vulnerability of girls, but many instances of the abuse of young boys are also depicted, that points out that no child is safe and thus some safeguards need to be thought about. Literature on prevention of child sexual abuse indicates that in many countries from a very young age, children are taught to respect their bodies. They are told about the good and the bad touch. In kindergarten itself children are taught that if someone tries to touch their body, or do things that make them feel unhappy or uncomfortable they should immediately say 'NO' to the person and report the incident to their parents.

Pinki Virani in her book *Bitter Chocolate* captures the situation and trauma related to child sexual abuse in India. Based on studies, reports and investigation, she reveals that a minimum 20 per cent of girls and boys under the age of 16 are being sexually abused regularly; half of them in their own homes, by adults who have the child's trust. Thus there is an immediate need to address the issue of child sexual abuse in India.

An abuser mostly is a known person with whom the child shares a comfort zone. The predator could be anybody an uncle, aunt, tutor, neighbour or a close relative. An abuser knows his or her game well. He or she lures the child into his or her secret game. A child who knows and cares for the abuser gets trapped into a game of affection and loyalty, with a sense that something is terribly wrong with the game. If the child tries to leak away the little secret game he or she may be threatened by violence or loss of love. Sometimes the child is also scared of the fact that nobody would believe him. Moreover, the realization that one has been abused comes much later, when one is older and fills the person with a range of negative emotions, associations and feelings of self-doubt.

Another dimension of child sexual abuse, which needs immediate attention, is the stigmatization attached with it. Child sexual abuse is surrounded by secrecy and is a tabooed issue. In fact, a lot of traditional beliefs and practices, particularly home and family seem to promote child sexual abuse. Sometimes the socio-economic conditions also make many children vulnerable and at a greater risk of getting sexually abused. In homes, many a times the child is not believed; at other times the parents don't want the family secret to go out. And so, cases of child sexual abuse, which are not severe, are seldom reported. There is no concern about what the victim is experiencing. More importance is given to preserving family name and identity.

Even in cases where the parents get over the shame and denial and the case is reported, there is no specific law against child sexual abuse. It is dealt with under various other laws like child rights and human rights. Sometimes the parents don't want to expose their children to the legal courts and their workings. Also the cases can go on for ages without a judgment. That further gives an advantage to the abuser, knowing that legal action against him will not be forthcoming.

In such a context it is important that appropriate interventions are required to address the issue of child sexual abuse in our country. Both family and schools can have a significant role in prevention of sexual abuse of children. Many times it is the family member, who is the abuser of a child; school becomes the only agent of appropriate intervention.

The present article tries to throw some light on the glaring issue of child sexual abuse in India. It explains the meaning and various dimensions of child sexual abuse as discussed by various sources of literature and media. The paper emphasizes the significant role of schools in addressing the various aspects of child sexual abuse from a preventive as well as promotive lens.

### What is Child Sexual Abuse?

Before discussing the role of school in prevention of sexual abuse of children and suggesting some ways towards its prevention and towards promotion of well being of children, one needs to understand the meaning of the term child sexual abuse (CSA) and all its dimensions.

There is no universal definition of child sexual abuse. It has been defined and interpreted in various ways. Child sexual abuse refers to any sexual behaviour directed at a person less than sixteen years of age without that person's informed consent. Sexual behaviour may include touching parts of the child or requesting the child to touch oneself, itself or others; ogling the child in a sexual manner, taking pornographic photographs, or requiring the child look at parts of the body, sexual acts or other material in a way which is arousing to oneself. It also includes verbal comments or suggestions to the child, which are intended to threaten the child sexually or otherwise to provide sexual gratification for one. It needs to be defined by and understood by the situation, circumstances and contexts in which it occurs: in families, in state-run and private institutions, on the street, in classrooms, in pornography, advertising and films. (Driver and Droisen, 1989)

*A Study on Child Abuse: India 2007*, done by the Ministry of Women and Child Development, Government of India conceptualizes sexual abuse as being severe in form and nature or assuming other forms which are less intensive, but definitely forms of sexual abuse.

In this conceptualization, the severe forms of sexual abuse include:

a) Assault, including rape and sodomy;

b) Touching or fondling a child;
c) Exhibitionism—forcing a child to exhibit his/her private body parts
d) Photographing a child in the nude.

The other forms of sexual abuse include:

a) Forcible kissing;
b) Sexual advances towards a child during travel;
c) Sexual advances towards a child during marriage situations;
d) Exhibitionism—exhibiting before a child;
e) Exposing a child to pornographic materials.

Sexual abuse is defined here as inappropriate sexual behaviour with a child. It includes fondling a child's genitals, intercourse, incest, rape, sodomy, exhibitionism and sexual exploitation. To be considered 'child sexual abuse', these acts have to be committed by a person responsible for the care of a child (for example baby-sitter, a parent or a day-care provider), or related to the child. If a stranger commits these acts, it would be considered sexual assault and handled solely by the police and criminal courts.

As defined by the World Health Organization, child sexual abuse is the involvement of a child in sexual activity that he or she does not fully comprehend, is unable to give informed consent to, or that violates the laws or social taboos of society. Child sexual abuse is evidenced by any such activity between a child and an adult, or another child who by age or development is in a relationship of responsibility, trust or power and the activity being intended to gratify or satisfy the needs of the person. This may include but is not limited to:

- The inducement or coercion of a child to engage in any unlawful activity
- The exploitative use of a child in prostitution or other unlawful sexual practices
- The exploitative use of children in pornographic performances and materials.

The Child Abuse Prevention and Treatment Act (CAPTA) defines the term sexual abuse as, "the employment, use, persuasion, inducement, enticement, or coercion of any child to engage in, or assist any other person to engage in, any sexually explicit conduct or simulation of such conduct for the purpose of producing a visual depiction of such conduct; or the rape, and in cases of caretaker or inter-familial relationships, statutory rape, molestation, prostitution, or other form of sexual exploitation of children, or incest with children."

What is common to all the conceptualizations and definitions is the fact that child sexual abuse includes activities by a parent or caretaker such as fondling a child's genitals, penetration, rape, sodomy, indecent exposure and exploitation through prostitution, or the production of pornographic materials in which the child typically remains a hapless victim.

The nature and intensity of child sexual abuse can vary considerably and it is thus important to classify it into some interpretive categories, in terms of the form it assumes and who the victim and offender are. Based on the readings that I have done the following may be an apt classification.

*Child Sexual Abuse as Sexual Assault*: It refers to any forced or coerced sexual intercourse or contact. This includes sexual molestation, sexual exploitation and sexual grooming of a child.

*Child Sexual Abuse as Incest*: This is explained as a culturally prohibited sexual relationship (up to and including coitus) between family members, such as a brother and sister or a parent and child. In case of child sexual abuse it is incest when a close adult relative is sexually abusing the child.

*Child Sexual Abuse as Paedophilia*: It is a paraphilia in which an adult's preferred or exclusive sexual partner is a pre-pubertal child. It is important to emphasize that paedophilia is defined by the bodily maturity, not the age, of the preferred partner. Thus studies of child sexual abuse, which typically define childhood based on an age range that may extend well into adolescence, do not necessarily concern paedophilia.

## Consequences of Child Sexual Abuse

Research studies have shown that sexual abuse during childhood can have seriously damaging impact on an individual. Some of the consequences can last a lifetime. The consequences of child sexual abuse are wide ranging and vary from survivor to survivor depending on a number of different factors such as the age of the victim, the duration and severity of the abuse, the number of perpetrators and the nature of the relationship with the perpetrator. However, it has a deep and long lasting impact on an individual's body and psyche. It leaves an individual with many consequences to bear and cope with. As listed by Laura Berk (2006) and other authors they can be summarized as follows:

- Depression, low self-esteem, mistrust of adults and anger and hostility can persist for years after the abusive episode.
- Younger children frequently react with sleep difficulties, loss of appetite and generalized fearfulness.
- Adolescents may run away and show suicidal reactions, substance abuse and delinquency.
- Sexually abused children frequently display sexual knowledge and behaviour beyond their age. They have learnt from their

abuser that sexual overtures are acceptable ways to get attention and rewards.

- In adolescence, abused young people often become promiscuous and are at risk of early childbearing and sexually transmitted diseases.
- In adulthood, child sexual abuse is related to increased arrest rates for sex crimes and prostitution.
- Women who are sexually abused are likely to choose partners who abuse them and their children. As mothers they often engage in irresponsible and coercive parenting, including child abuse and neglect. In these ways the harmful impact of child sexual abuse is transmitted to the next generation.

**Indicators of Child Sexual Abuse**

The very first step towards providing appropriate intervention is to identify a child who is being sexually abused. When a child is sexually abused he or she undergoes certain physical and behavioural changes, which act as indicators of child sexual abuse. They are classified as physical and behavioural indicators respectively and are as follows:

*Physical Indicators*

- Torn, stained or bloodied underclothing.
- Pain or itching in throat, anal or genital area.
- Genital, urethral or anal trauma
- Recurrent abdominal pain
- Difficulty walking or sitting
- Bruises or bleeding in external genetalia
- Veneral diseases
- Frequent urinary or yeast infections
- Pregnancy

*Behavioural Indicators*

- Confusion
- Withdrawn, anxiety, chronic depression
- Deep sense of isolation
- Bed- wetting beyond a certain age
- Avoiding certain adults
- Constant rubbing of body parts against objects
- Temper tantrums
- Excessive seductiveness
- Role reversal, overly concerned for siblings
- Poor self-esteem, self-devaluation, lack of confidence

- Peer problems, lack of involvement
- Massive weight changes
- Substance abuse
- Inability to eat certain foods that resemble the male organ or semen
- Suicide attempts (especially in adolescents)
- Hysteria, lack of emotional control
- Sudden school difficulties
- Inappropriate sex play or premature understanding of sex
- Threatened by physical contact or closeness
- Promiscuity.

A sexually abused child may have many or none of these signs or indicators. Not every child with these signs is abused, but these indicators should be investigated further.

**Schools as Preventive Spaces**

All discourse on School Mental Health perceives school as the most potent context to promote the psychological well being of the growing child. The WHO (1989, 91) and Malvika Kapur, (1997, 2007) one of the leading persons in Mental Health in India, have time and again emphasized that rather than waiting for mental illness and then engaging in cure, it is much better to anticipate some difficulties and problems in advance, based on research trends, what clinical practice reveals and take preventive action in schools. Sensitization, awareness generation and actual coping education are all possible to give and achieve, through the larger canvas of school education. Also, since school is a microcosm of society and the place where children spend maximum hours of alert wakefulness, it is a very appropriate setting for addressing all issues in education. Children come to learn, live and share experiences and get opportunities to seek answers to many questions, which occupy their minds. Homes are often uncomfortable in dealing with personal and psycho-social issues and very often, children's queries and experiences in these spheres, remain unaddressed.

It was in this context that schools might be considered the most appropriate spaces where this issue of child sexual abuse can be dealt with, from a prevention lens. School is the most significant social institution, outside the family, with which children have consistent, ongoing interaction. Moreover, since schools shoulder the responsibility of promoting the all round development of a child, so that he or she can adjust better to the changing dynamics of society, there would be no better place than the school.

Case studies of children who have been sexually abused show both long-term and short-term adverse effects on the mind and body of a child hampering his/her normal growth. Sometimes children are seen to develop behavioural problems due to this. It is thus imperative for schools to have some programs and strategies to make parents and children aware of child sexual abuse.

Furthermore, since most of the times the perpetrator is a close relative or a family friend that the family trusts, the child cannot turn to the family for support. In such cases, school becomes the sole saviour of the child. Therefore it is important for schools to have some intervention strategies to deal with identification, counselling and restoration of the well being of an affected child. Considerable focus has been given to this aspect in my research.

Indian media too has tried depicting the phenomenon of child sexual abuse in our society through films, discussion programmes and chat shows. Movies in particular, show how the effects of child sexual abuse haunt the victims even in their adulthood. One can imagine the agony they went through over all those years closely guarding the darkest secret of their lives. Media has thus contributed towards bringing child sexual abuse into public discourse and so it is time that this issue is taken up by mainstream schools. Needless to reiterate the fact that school is a near universal experience in every child's life. Schools can play a significant role in dealing with this issue and it would therefore be worthwhile to know their perspective and attitude towards their potential role in this regard. Studies in Mental Health have emphasized the preventive dimension of intervention and that child sexual abuse could be dealt with through a preventive approach. Due to the overarching focus on it a framework for schools is suggested in the next section, to help schools in dealing with issues of child sexual abuse.

### Preventive Framework for Schools

The school equips the child with skills that would help him/her to adjust well in his or her environment. Child sexual abuse is a threat to a child's proper all round development. It has a long lasting impact on a child's psyche. Sometimes it might lead to socially deviant behavior. Thus it is important for schools to have a programme that would not only provide healing intervention to the victims, but also help to prevent the incidence of child sexual abuse. Following is a suggested programme framework, aimed at helping schools in addressing issues of child sexual abuse. The schools can come up with their own frameworks based on their school's individual needs, using the following suggestions.

### Programme Outline

Any qualitative programme is not a one-time affair; it should be an ongoing process catering to all the students of the school. It should be updated each year according to the changes taking place in society and the availability of better information sources. First and foremost the school principal and teacher need to be oriented to the issue of child sexual abuse, its severity and the need for preventive measures. Schools should be willing to make prevention of child sexual abuse a part of their school curricular and co-curricular activities.

However, schools have their own limitations. They cannot take all the decisions about their students; it is important that the consent of the parents is there as well. Schools should thus organize orientation workshops where they can sensitize parents about child sexual abuse. They can explain the need for a programme for the prevention of child sexual abuse to the parents. Professionals could be invited to orient parents. The Parent teacher association can be an apt platform for discussing the issue with parents.

Usually schools have one counselor who cannot deal with the vast multitude of problems of all the students of the school. Equally important is the fact that it is the teachers who spend more time in the class than the counselor. Therefore, teachers and counselors should both be made a part of this programme.

For any such programme to be successful it is imperative that teachers and counselors are prepared to deal with cases of child sexual abuse. The teachers and counselors should be given proper orientation in this regard. The counselor should be professionally trained to deal with the abuse problems of children from diagnosis to healing.

It is suggested that the programme have three levels, in accordance with the age group of the students and the level stratification structure, which is adopted by schools.

*a) Primary Level*

In a school primary level includes learners from classes one to five. But pre-primary students can also be included in this level.

At this level child sexual abuse can be made a part of the health and hygiene programme, which is already going on in many schools. In this programme the teachers tell students about different body parts and ways to keep them healthy and clean. The students can be provided age appropriate information about child sexual abuse during these classes. The teachers of some schools do teach students about the good touch and the bad touch. But they need to go beyond this. While telling them about their body parts, teachers should introduce students to the names of the body parts. Teacher can tell the students that they have full right on their bodies and if anybody be it a stranger or a known person, does anything that makes them feel funny, weird or bad, they should ask the person to stop doing it. They should also then tell an elder, parent or teacher about the experience.

A few schools organize parenting workshops. In such workshops along with other topics, parents should be sensitized towards the issue of child sexual abuse. Parents should encourage their children to discuss various issues with them right from childhood. They should be trained in the art of active listening. This would help in the development of a home environment that is conducive to sharing.

Different subject teachers can incorporate the issue into their classroom topics. Language teachers can build stories on child sexual abuse; science teacher can introduce the topic to students while teaching them about their bodies. Similarly, social science teacher can talk about this topic while talking about types of home and safety rules.

*b) Middle Level*

This level includes students from class six to eight. This is the period of the onset of puberty. Students undergo a lot of bodily changes. It includes hormonal changes and development of secondary sex characteristics.

Schools have life skills programmes at this level to enable students to life challenges. Child sexual abuse can be made a part of the life skills programme. Teachers can discuss the topic openly in the class. They should encourage students to discuss their problems. An open sharing based classroom would build a bond of trust between the teacher and students. The students would easily be able to approach the teacher with their problems. This would help bringing out the cases of child sexual abuse from the closet. The teacher could organize talk sessions on the topic of child sexual abuse. This would help the students in understanding the issue. Many children undergoing sexual abuse fail to understand what is going on with them. The child might think that something unusual and bad is happening to him or her that he or she cannot share with anybody. A clear description of child sexual abuse will help the child in understanding what is happening to him or her and evolve ways to deal with it.

The issue can be weaved into different subjects like science, language and social studies. Students could be asked to write short stories or essays on the topic. While teaching the reproductive system, the issue can be introduced and explained to the learners.

*c) Secondary and Senior Secondary Level*

This level includes students from class nine to twelve. By this time students have attained puberty. Schools have adolescence education programmes to sensitize students about the problems related to adolescence. These include interpersonal relations, sexuality, reproduction, and career choices etc. Child sexual abuse can be made part of this programme. The teacher could discuss the issue with students. The teacher could tell students about the different effects of child sexual abuse on the psyche of a child and ways to deal with the emerging emotions and conflict.

At this level, learners are mature enough so the teacher can discuss this topic openly with them. The teacher can discuss the case stories of survivors of child sexual abuse. There are many famous personalities who have been victims of sexual abuse in their childhood. Such examples could be discussed in the class to show that everyone can move pass a traumatic incident and rebuild his or her life.

In different subjects too the issue can be incorporated and elaborated upon. Social science gets divided into history, geography and civics. History teachers can discuss the social context of child sexual abuse. They can explain to students why the issue is so less talked about in our society and why victims do not report it. Psychology teachers can orient the students to the various effects of child sexual abuse on an individual.

**Suggested Activities**

A number of activities can be organized in school to sensitize students about the topic of child sexual abuse. These could include:

- Essay writing
- Story writing
- Painting
- Collage making
- Awareness drives
- Students rallies
- Plays
- Skits
- Professional addresses
- Workshops
- Seminars

Newspaper cuttings on the topic of child sexual abuse could be put up on the school bulletin boards. Stories and write-ups on the issue can be published in the school newspaper and magazine. Literature related to child sexual abuse could be made available in the library. Films related to the issue can be screened in the schools followed by a talk session.

The issue needs to be discussed with students, among teachers and with parents. This would help remove the stigma attached to it. This will enable students to understand it better. Students who are being sexually abused would be able to report it to teachers and parents. This would help school counselors to identify cases of child sexual abuse. Appropriate and timely intervention can then be provided to the abused child.

Many schools have doctors or they collaborate with hospitals for health check-ups and other medical issues concerning students. In a similar stead, schools can have a tie-up with doctors and mental health professionals to whom they can refer cases of severe trauma and behavioral problems. Help line numbers and numbers of organizations working in the area of prevention of child sexual abuse should also be made available to the students and their parents.

Most of the time when a child discloses being sexually abused to the teacher, there is nothing more than counseling that a teacher or counselor can do. In cases where one of the parents is an abuser or where the family does not want to report the case, a teacher can do nothing to help the child. There should be a reporting system where such cases can be reported. There should be a medico-legal support system for all the schools. It should have all types of experts like lawyers, psychologists, psychiatrists, non-government organizations etc.

### Conclusion

Child sexual abuse is a reality of our society, whether we want to accept it or not. As we have discussed already, it has a long lasting impact on the mind and body of an individual. There are a lot of behavioral problems which an individual can fall prey to, as a result of sexual abuse during child hood. In the face of this reality, one can understand the urgent need to develop strategies to identify and address cases of child sexual abuse. A lot can be done to curb the evil of child sexual abuse from our society. Accepting the reality and willingness to fight, are initial steps towards achieving the goal. Families and schools need to come together and work co-operatively to protect their children from getting sexually abused.

Schools play an important part in a child's life. People often reminisce about the memories of their school life. The role of school is important in the all round development of a child. Schools should provide a safe and healthy environment to a child that is conducive for learning. Child sexual abuse cannot be made the sole area of attention in schools but it could be made a part of different ongoing programmes. Parents and teachers can share the responsibility. They can take the first step by providing a classroom and home environment conducive to open sharing. It is time that this issue comes out of closed doors and gets discussed at a public level.

## REFERENCES

Berk, L.E. (2007). Child Development, 7th ed, Pearson Education, Delhi, Prentice Hall, pp.587- 591

Dutta, S. (2009). Incest, Child Abuse is India's Hidden Shame. Retrieved December 25, 2011, http://www.merinews.com/article/incest-child-abuse-is-indias-hidden-shame/15760077.shtml

Kapur, M. (1997). Mental Health in Indian Schools. New Delhi: Sage Publication.

Government of India, Ministry of Women and Child Development (2007). *Study on Child Abuse INDIA,* New Delhi: Kriti.

Santrock, J.W. (2007). Adolescence, 11th ed, New Delhi, Tata McGraw Hill edition, pp 225-230

SCERT (2009). *YUVA School Life-Skills Programme, Course designed for Training of teachers,* Department of Education, New Delhi.

Vasudev, S. (2002). *Innocence Vioated.* Retrieved December 25, 2011, http://www.indiatoday.com/itoday/20021118/society.shtml

Virani, P. (2000). Bitter Chocolate: Child Sexual Abuse in India. India: Penguin Books.

Wadhwa, S. (1997). *To Think the Unthinkable.* Retrieved December 25, 2011, http://www.outlookindia.com/article.aspx?203966

Wolfe, D.A. (1999). *Child Abuse Implications for Child Development and Psychopathology*, 2nd ed., Thousand Oaks, CA: Sage Publication

WHO (2002). *The World Health Report- 2002*, World Health Organization, Geneva: Switzerland

# 11

# Education, Gender, Access and Participation to Elementary Education

## *Bundelkhand Region of Uttar Pradesh*

***Manju Narula***

Uttar Pradesh (UP) is one of the largest and most populous states in the country accounting for 16.4 per cent of the country's population of which 80 per cent of the population lives in rural areas. It had 70 districts, 962 blocks and 85654 villages according to the Census 2001. The state has made substantial progress since independence but continues to be among the most economically and educationally backward, states of the country.

Universalization of Elementary Education is Constitutional Commitment and one of national agenda. But, the state is far from achieving the goal of universalization of elementary education. The literacy rate in general and female literacy in particular continues to be low. Its literacy rate (57.36 percent) is low than national average (65.38 percent) as per the Census 2001. There is a wide gap between male and female literacy rates. The gap between male and female literacy is 27.25 per cent points. Male literacy is 70.23 per cent while female literacy rate is 42.98 per cent. Out of 35 states and Union Territories the rank of U.P. is 31st on overall literacy, 30th on male literacy and 32nd on female literacy. There is wide inter-district variation in the literacy rates. In some of the districts literacy rate is below 50 per cent and female literacy rate is below 30 per cent. The Gross enrolment ratio (GRE) at the primary level in the state is 112.9 per cent and GRE at upper primary level is 47.2 (2006-07), with the rate varying widely across districts and between sexes. Many interventions have been made to bridge these gaps. These include the transfer of primary and upper primary schools to the Panchayati Raj Institutions (PRIs) as a step towards decentralization of management, in consonance with the 73rd constitutional amendment. To address the problem of teacher shortage para teachers were appointed locally on contract basis. Very pronounced interventions to address the educational backwardness in the state were made under the projects like: Uttar Pradesh Basic Education Project (UPBEP) and District Primary Education Programme (DPEP). UPBEP-I approved in 1993, designed to expand access to elementary schools, especially of socially disadvantaged groups, to improve student learning and enhance capacity to manage elementary education in 17 educationally backward districts. DPEP in the second phase i.e. in 1996 covered 18 additional disadvantaged districts of the state and again UPBEP II approved in 1997 to address the upsurge of enrolment growths in the 17 districts. As a result of implementing these programmes enrolment had increased substantially. However, the increase in enrolment has resulted in unacceptable large classes and acute shortages of teachers and classrooms. Other interventions are centrally sponsored schemes like Non formal education, Operational Blackboard, and Sarva Shiksha Abhiyan (SSA) to improve the access, retention and to reduce dropout rates.

The state of Uttar Pradesh is divided into four economic regions namely—Western, Central, Eastern and Bundelkhand. There are significant inter-regional disparities in respect of development indicators among these four regions. These development indicators were on the basis of industrial infrastructure, economic infrastructure and social infrastructure (Singh 2006). Out of them paper concentrates only social and some of economic indicators (Table 11.1). The Table shows that though Central region has relatively less area, but it has high density of population. It has generally been found that less developed regions have often-difficult topography, low development of infrastructure facilities like roads, electrification, schools, etc. Eastern UP accounts highest population growth, lowest urbanization, 40 per cent of state's population live in the region, it has relatively less total literacy than the state's literacy, female literacy is also low in comparison with other regions of UP. On the other hand, Bundelkhand region has difficult topography, lowest electrification of villages and lowest road connectivity. The region has very less population, less area per square kilometer, less density of population and lowest literacy rate. In Bundelkhand region the total literacy rate and female literacy rates both are lowest in comparison with all the regions. It is perhaps because of relatively lower population growth and low density of population in Bundelkhand Region the availability of primary and upper primary schools per lakh population is more here when compared with other regions. However only the number of schools does not ensure the educational development of the region and other indicators like participation of children, availability of teachers, facilities in schools, performance of students are important in this regard.

**Table 11.1: Region-wise Development Indicators of UP, 2001**

| *Variables* | *Eastern* | *Western* | *Central* | *Bundelkhand* | *UP* |
|---|---|---|---|---|---|
| Population (000') | 66628 (40.09%) | 61114 (36.78%) | 30201 (18.17%) | 8232 (4.96%) | 166175 (100%) |
| Area Sq.Km. | 85845 (33.13%) | 79831 (33.13%) | 45834 (19.03%) | 29418 (12.21%) | 240928 (100%) |
| Density of Population | 776 | 767 | 658 | 280 | 690 |
| Population growth 1991-2001 (%) | 26.35 | 26.05 | 24.73 | 22.32 | 25.80 |
| per cent Urban population in 2001 | 11.78 | 28.25 | 25.11 | 22.46 | 20.78 |
| P.C. NSDP 1999-2000 at current prices in rupees | 6995 | 12385 | 9637 | 9267 | 9765 |
| per cent villages electrified in 2000-01 | 77.90 | 88.81 | 72.55 | 69.94 | 79.27 |
| Length of roads per 1000 sq. km. area in 2001 | 440.31 | 455.41 | 387.66 | 279.97 | 415.63 |
| Literacy per cent (2001) | 55.22 | 58.44 | 59.04 | 48.41 | 57.36 |
| Female Literacy per cent (2001) | 39.54 | 44.64 | 47.12 | 34.98 | 42.98 |
| Primary Schools per lakh population in 2003-04 | 62 | 72 | 67 | 98 | 63 |
| Upper Primary Schools per lakh population in 2003-04 | 19 | 21 | 19 | 33 | 20 |

The present paper is confined to Bundelkhand region of Uttar Pradesh It is divided into four parts: first part talks about the present educational situation. The second part diagnoses the causes of low literacy rate and educational development in terms of access, participation and quality at elementary level. The third part points out the efforts by the government to achieve the goal of universalization of elementary education (UEE) and finally concludes by giving suggestions to overcome the difficulties in achieving the goals of UEE. Data is collected from the secondary sources like Elementary Education in India, progress towards UEE- District Information System on Education; District Report Cards, Elementary Education in India, Where do we stand?; Selected Educational Statistics of Ministry of Human Resource Development, and Annual Plans of the districts. In addition views of official from the districts and NGO's were also taken, in various forums.

The Bundelkhand region of Central India is a semi-arid plateau that encompasses 10 districts of northern Madhya Pradesh (MP) and 7 districts of southern Uttar Pradesh (UP). It is located in the central Hindi belt south of the Yamuna river, between the fertile Gangetic plain stretching across northern UP and the highlands of central MP. Bundelkhand region is an old landmass composed of horizontal rock beds resting on a stable foundation. The landscape is rugged, featuring undulating terrain with low rocky outcrops, narrow valleys, and plains.

### Demographic Features of Bundelkhand Region

The total population of Bundelkhand region of U.P. was 82 lakh according to Census 2001 (see Table 11.2). The region consists of seven districts: Banda, Hamirpur, Jhansi, Mahoba, Lalitpur, Chitrakoot and Jalaun. Most populous district is Jhansi (17 lakh), followed by Banda (15 lakh), Jalaun (14 lakh), Hamirpur (10 lakh), Lalitpur (97 lakh), Chitrakoot (76 lakh) and Mahoba (7 lakh). In this region more than 75 per cent of the population lives in rural areas, except Jhansi district. Among all the districts, Lalitpur district has highest rural population i.e. 85.09 per cent and lowest rural population is in Jhansi district (58.92 per cent). The Schedule Caste (SC) population ranges from 8.66 per cent to 18.22 per cent in all the districts of the region.

**Table 11.2 : Demographic Profile of Bundelkhand Region, 2001**

| *Bundelkhand Districts* | *Total population* | *Total per cent of population* | *Total per cent Rural of Population* | *Total per cent of SC Population* |
|---|---|---|---|---|
| Banda | 1537334 | .90 | 83.73 | 14.25 |
| Hamirpur | 1043724 | .63 | 83.36 | 14.89 |
| Jhansi | 1744931 | 1.05 | 58.92 | 18.22 |
| Mahoba | 0708447 | 8.43 | 71.16 | 8.66 |
| Lalitpur | 0977734 | .50 | 85.09 | 25.08 |
| Chitrakoot | 0766225 | .48 | 83.36 | 8.72 |
| Jalaun | 1454452 | .88 | 76.61 | 17.35 |
| Total | 8232847 | | | |

*Source*: Census 2001

### Literacy Scenario

Literacy rate is the most basic indicator of a country's educational development. There is clear evidence that literacy raises the productivity and earning potential of a population, and improves the quality of life. Yet, illiteracy is widespread problem in most of the states in India. In case of Bundelkhand region of U.P. more than half the population of the region is without any literacy skills. Literacy rates show that all the districts of the region have lower literacy in comparison to national literacy rates

(65.38 per cent). Female literacy is considered to be a more sensitive index of social development compared to overall literacy rates. Female literacy rate is negatively related with fertility rates, population growth rates, and infant and child mortality rates and show a positive association with female age at marriage, life expectancy, and with female enrolments. Yet, about only one third females (34.98 per cent), are literates in the region. Lalitpur district has lowest female literacy rate (26.02 per cent) among all the districts of the region. It looks very strange that 74 per cent of the females are illiterate in the district (see Figure 11.1).

**Figure 11.1: Education Profile of Bundelkhand District**

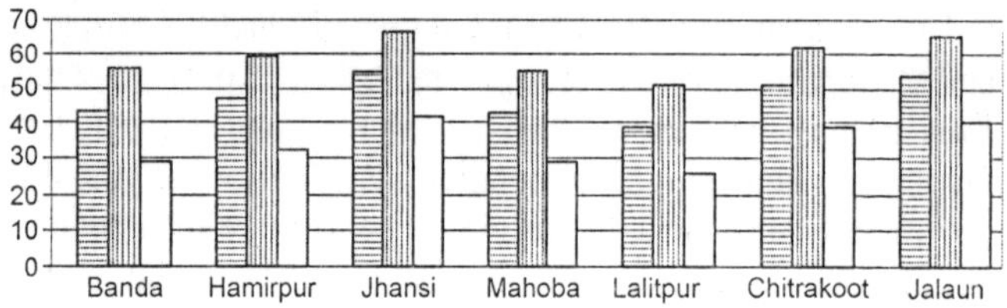


| | Banda | Hamirpur | Jhansi | Mahoba | Lalitpur | Chitrakoot | Jalaun |
|---|---|---|---|---|---|---|---|
| Total Literate % | 43.64 | 47 | 54.94 | 43.14 | 39.3 | 51.29 | 52.76 |
| Male Literate % | 56.01 | 59.22 | 66.19 | 55.09 | 51.06 | 61.74 | 64.77 |
| Female Literate % | 20.26 | 32.64 | 42.02 | 29.33 | 26.02 | 39.31 | 40.8 |

*Source*: Census 2001, GOI, New Delhi.

### Availability of Schooling Facilities

Table 11.3 shows that in spite of all the interventions by the government of India still there are 1676 villages of the region that does not have schooling facilities.

**Table 11.3: Villages without Schooling Facilities**

| | |
|---|---|
| Banda | 284 |
| Hamirpur | 188 |
| Jhansi | 467 |
| Mahoba | 121 |
| Lalitpur | 169 |
| Chitrakoot | 174 |
| Jalaun | 273 |
| Total | 1676 |

*Source*: 7th AIES, NCERT

### Access

Access is assessed on the basis of indicators like proportion of population served with schools by distance number of schools by per lakh of population, The Table 11.4 shows that by 2002, the state is providing more access to primary schools and upper primary schools in rural areas within the habitation, yet large areas are still without schooling facilities. Much effort is still needed to bring all the children to accommodate all the children into the schools.

**Table 11.4: Availability of Schooling Facilities in Habitations at Primary and Upper-primary Stages**

| | | Primary | | | Upper Primary | | |
|---|---|---|---|---|---|---|---|
| | *Total Habitations* | *Within them* | *Within 1 K.M.* | *Beyond 1 K.M.* | *Within them* | *Within 1 K.M.* | *Beyond 1 K.M.* |
| Banda | 1612 | 54.40 | 36.60 | 9.00 | 19.67 | 61.04 | 19.29 |
| Hamirpur | 1023 | 90.22 | 6.16 | 3.62 | 27.57 | 49.17 | 23.26 |
| Jhansi | 1046 | 71.80 | 14.82 | 13.38 | 20.75 | 43.12 | 36.14 |
| Mahoba | 1031 | 63.24 | 17.65 | 19.11 | 17.94 | 44.13 | 37.92 |
| Lalitpur | 518 | 85.91 | 8.88 | 5.21 | 23.55 | 29.15 | 47.30 |
| Chitrakoot | 1269 | 50.04 | 37.04 | 12.92 | 16.39 | 69.90 | 13.71 |
| Jalaun | 604 | 86.42 | 11.75 | 1.82 | 33.11 | 47.68 | 19.21 |

## Growth of Schools

The Table 11.5 shows that number of schools at the primary and upper primary levels, increased substantially in all the districts of Bundelkhand region of U.P. from 2001-02 to 2006-07. At the primary level the scenario of growth of schools reveals that in Hamirpur, Banda and Lalitpur districts annual average growth rate of schools was more in comparison to Bundelkhand region (6.58 percent) and in Jalaun districts annually near about 15 per cent primary schools increased. Lowest growth rate of schools for primary level is observed in Chitrakoot district (3.03 per cent).

**Table 11. 5: Average Annual Growth Rate of Schools at Primary and Upper Primary Levels in Bundelkhand Region**

| | *Banda* | *Hamir-pur* | *Jhansi* | *Mahoba* | *Lalit pur* | *Chitra koot* | *Jalaun* | *Total Bundelkhand* |
|---|---|---|---|---|---|---|---|---|
| Primary Schools | | | | | | | | |
| 2001-02 | 897 | 585 | 1192 | 579 | 756 | 764 | 1184 | 5957 |
| 2006-07 | 1429 | 1052 | 1425 | 767 | 1061 | 887 | 1572 | 8193 |
| AAGR | 9.76 | 12.45 | 3.64 | 5.78 | 7.01 | 3.03 | 5.83 | 6.58 |
| Upper primary Schools | | | | | | | | |
| 2001-02 | 396 | 235 | 285 | 135 | 189 | 230 | 831 | 2301 |
| 2004-05 | 598 | 523 | 695 | 364 | 428 | 363 | 726 | 3697 |
| AAGR | 8.59 | 17.35 | 19.52 | 21.94 | 17.76 | 9.56 | -2.67 | 9.95 |

*Source*: Selected Educational Statistics, 2001-02, MHRD, New Delhi and DISE 2006-07, NUEPA, New Delhi.

At the upper primary level Hamirpur, Jhansi, Mahoba and Lalitpur districts observed more annual average growth rate of schools than overall of Bundelkhand region. Because of the interventions by the state government and SSA programme more number of schools may have been opened. In Jalaun district negative annual growth rate is observed. The reason may be good number of upper primary schools may also been up-graded to secondary schools.

**Participation at Elementary Level**

Among the more commonly used measures to see the participation of students are growth of enrolment, gross enrolment ratio, and net enrolment ratio.

**Enrolment Trends:** The Table 11.6 shows the annual increase of primary and upper primary enrolment in Bundelkhand Region of U.P. The annual average growth rate of enrolment at primary level was observed more among the Bundelkhand region in Banda, Mahoba, Chitrakoot and Jalaun districts. The district Banda experienced highest average annual growth rate (10.33 per cent). Lowest average annual growth rate of children at primary level was found in Jhansi district (3.12 per cent).

However growth of number of children was slightly better at upper primary level as compared to primary level. Average annual growth rate of the region was 14.03 per cent. The number of children at upper primary level increased from lowest 10.33 per cent to highest 20.97 per cent annually in the 7 districts of Bundelkhand Region of U.P. Highest annual growth rate was observed in Chitrakoot (20.97 per cent) and lowest was experienced in Mahoba district (10.33 per cent).

**Table 11.6: Average Annual Growth Rate of Enrolment at Primary and Upper Primary Levels in Bundelkhand Region of U.P.**

| | *Banda* | *Hamir-pur* | *Jhansi* | *Mahoba* | *Lalit pur* | *Chitra koot* | *Jalaun* | *Total* |
|---|---|---|---|---|---|---|---|---|
| Primary Enrolment | | | | | | | | |
| 2002-03 | 189005 | 130605 | 206546 | 103061 | 150572 | 105302 | 177108 | 1062199 |
| 2006-07 | 280057 | 168643 | 233514 | 133954 | 195268 | 154125 | 243743 | 1409304 |
| AAGR | 10.33 | 6.60 | 3.12 | 6.77 | 6.71 | 9.99 | 8.31 | 7.32 |
| Upper-primary Enrolment | | | | | | | | |
| 2002-03 | 34871 | 29434 | 47526 | 24436 | 32792 | 16631 | 34875 | 220565 |
| 2006-07 | 71574 | 53807 | 79140 | 39957 | 56036 | 43079 | 81722 | 425315 |
| AAGR | 15.47 | 12.82 | 10.74 | 10.33 | 11.31 | 20.97 | 18.57 | 14.03 |

Source: DISE, NUEPA, 2006-07, New Delhi

**Gross Enrolment Ratio (GER)** is indicative of the general level of participation of children at a given grade or level of education. The Table

11.7 shows that GER at primary and upper primary levels have significantly improved during 2004-05 to 2006-07. GER in 2006-07 is found more than 100 per cent in all districts except Jhansi. Though in Jhansi district during 2005-06 GER was 100 per cent, in the subsequent year it has slightly declined.

However at the upper primary level participation of students is very unsatisfactory. In spite of accounting for over age and under age children GER in 2006-07 in Hamirpur, Lalitpur and Chitrakoot is even less than 20 per cent. Some concentrated efforts are needed to bring all the children in the preview of education at upper primary level.

**Table 11.7: GER at Primary level and Upper Primary level**

| *Name of the Districts* | *2004-05* | | *2005-06* | | *2006-07* | |
|---|---|---|---|---|---|---|
| | *Primary GER* | *Upper Primary GER* | *Primary GER* | *Upper Primary GER* | *Primary GER* | *Upper Primary GER* |
| Banda | 94.5 | 39.0 | 127.0 | 51.3 | 133.2 | 45.3 |
| Hamirpur | 90.5 | 46.2 | 115.8 | 58.6 | 118.2 | 15.2 |
| Jhansi | 84.7 | 46.6 | 101.5 | 52.4 | 97.9 | 53.9 |
| Mahoba | 103.0 | 48.4 | 129.7 | 56.8 | 138.3 | 20.1 |
| Lalitpur | 106.4 | 51.1 | 140.7 | 62.4 | 146.1 | 14.2 |
| Chitrakoot | 108.4 | 40.4 | 138.8 | 55.6 | 147.1 | 12.6 |
| Jalaun | 88.4 | 39.6 | 114.5 | 59.8 | 122.6 | 20.7 |

*Source*: DISE, NUEPA, 2006-07, New Delhi

## Gender Equity

Studies have shown that educational backwardness is one of the factors associated with social and economic deprivation and vice-versa. The districts covered under Bundelkhand region of U.P. are characterized by persistence of high gender inequities. Female literacy rate is observed very low (34.98 percent) in the region. The status of girl's education in the region is depicted in the Table 7. The Table shows that whether girls are at primary level or upper primary their enrolment is less than 40 per cent. Within the districts there are disparities for girls's enrolment. At the primary level girls's enrolment varies from 29.70 per cent to 38.72 per cent. At the upper primary level it varies from 24.87 per cent to 34.76 per cent. In Jhansi and Jalaun districts more number of girl's are at the primary level in comparison to other districts of Bundelkhand region of U.P. Lowest enrolment of girl's at the primary level was in Lalitpur district i.e. 29.70 per cent and at the upper primary level in Mahoba district i.e. 24.87 per cent. It may be pertinent to point out that in Bundelkhand region there is demand for single sex schools for girls, especially among rural communities.

**Table 11.8: Status of Girls Enrolment in Bundelkhand Region of U.P. 2006-07**

| *Bundelkhand Region Name of the Districts* | *Primary Girls as per cent to Total Enrolment* | *Upper Primary Girls as per cent to Total Enrolment* |
|---|---|---|
| Banda | 32.92 | 33.96 |
| Hamirpur | 34.42 | 28.61 |
| Jhansi | 38.72 | 34.76 |
| Mahoba | 34.37 | 24.87 |
| Lalitpur | 29.70 | 25.27 |
| Chitrakoot | 31.23 | 28.74 |
| Jalaun | 38.82 | 31.63 |

*Source*: DISE, NUEPA, 2006-07, New Delhi

## Teachers

The Table 11.9 depicts average annual growth rate of teachers at primary level and upper primary levels. In Bundelkhand region at the primary level during 2001-02 there were 17600 primary teachers that increased to 25880 in 2005-06. 8 per cent average annual growth rate of primary teachers in 5 years in the region was observed. In 3 districts namely Banda, Hamirpur and Jhansi in comparison to the region, more average annual growth rate of primary teachers was noted i.e. 14.10 per cent, 13.94 per cent and 9.25 per cent respectively. However in Banda and Hamirpur

**Table 11.9: Average Annual Growth Rate of Teachers at Primary and Upper Primary Levels in Bundelkhand Region**

| | *Banda* | *Hamir- pur* | *Jhansi* | *Mahoba* | *Lalit pur* | *Chitra koot* | *Jalaun* | *Total Bundelkhand Region* |
|---|---|---|---|---|---|---|---|---|
| Primary Schools | | | | | | | | |
| 2001-02 | 2322 | 1850 | 3830 | 1896 | 2559 | 1507 | 3636 | 17600 |
| 2005-06 | 4490 | 3553 | 5962 | 2134 | 2818 | 2034 | 4889 | 25880 |
| AAGR | 14.10 | 13.94 | 9.25 | 2.39 | 1.95 | 6.18 | 6.10 | 8.02 |
| Upper-primary | | | | | | | | |
| 2001-02 | 999 | 841 | 1256 | 529 | 727 | 433 | 1457 | 6242 |
| 2005-06 | 1893 | 1173 | 2347 | 839 | 1060 | 983 | 3360 | 11655 |
| AAGR | 13.64 | 6.88 | 13.32 | 9.66 | 7.83 | 17.82 | 18.19 | 13.30 |

Selected Educational statistics, 2001-02 & 2004-05, MHRD, New Delhi districts average annual growth rate of teachers was substantial. On the other hand, in Mahoba, and Lalitpur districts annual growth rate of teachers was very low i.e. 2.39 per cent and 1.95 per cent respectively.

However, at the upper primary level from 2001-02 to 2005-06 teachers increased from 6247 to 11655. The average annual growth rate (13.30 percent) was large than primary school teachers. Highest average annual growth rate of upper primary teachers was found in Jalaun district followed by Chitrakoot district. Unlikely to Hamirpur district where average annual growth rate was higher for primary level, at upper primary level growth of teachers was lowest.

## Recruitment of Teachers

For the appointment of teachers, different states have adopted their own norms. However, Operational Blackboard recommended the appointment of a minimum of two teachers in each primary school. Whenever the enrolment exceeds 80-100, an additional teacher is provided. The Table 11.10 shows average number of teachers at the school level in Bundelkhand region of U.P. At the primary and upper primary levels average number of teacher ranges between 3 to 4 per school. Up to upper primary levels same situation exists except Lalitpur district. As far as in-service training of teachers is concerned situation in the region is not very encouraging, except Chitrakoot district at both the levels. In Mahoba district only 5.5 per cent of teachers received in-service training followed by Banda (11.0) and Lalitpur (11.7).

## Female Teachers

The Table 11.11 shows the share of female teachers to total teachers in Bundelkhand region of U.P. Women teachers are less than 20 per cent except Jhansi and Lalitpur at primary level. At upper primary level out of

**Table 11.10: Distribution of Average Number of Teachers District wise**

| | *Primary* | *Pry.+ U.P.* |
|---|---|---|
| Banda | 3.5 | 5.2 |
| Hamirpur | 3.4 | 5.5 |
| Jhansi | 3.8 | 4.7 |
| Mahoba | 3.2 | 5.9 |
| Lalitpur | 3.5 | 8.5 |
| Chitrakoot | 3.1 | 6.0 |
| Jalaun | 2.8 | 4.3 |

*Source*: DISE, NUEPA, 2006-07, New Delhi

7 districts in the region 3 districts women teachers are again less than 20 per cent. In Mahoba district women teachers are only 9 per cent. Research evidences show that low proportion of women teachers is one of the major reasons for low enrolment of girls at the primary and upper primary levels. To improve the girls participation in the region recruitment of more female teachers is required and special efforts are needed to promote girls education in these districts. According to the Operational Blackboard scheme each school should have a minimum of two teachers and one of these should preferably be a female teacher.

**Table 11.11: Share of Female Teachers to Total Teachers**

| *Bundelkhand Districts* | *Primary* | *Upper Primary* |
|---|---|---|
| Banda | 16.84 | 59.26 |
| Hamirpur | 18.40 | 16.32 |
| Jhansi | 37.70 | 34.19 |
| Mahoba | 16.76 | 9.19 |
| Lalitpur | 41.45 | 13.68 |
| Chitrakoot | 14.68 | 48.47 |
| Jalaun | 18.21 | 20.40 |

*Source*: DISE, NUEPA, 2006-07, New Delhi

## Quality of Education

To see the quality at primary and upper primary levels pass percentage at the terminal examination is seen. The Table 11.12 shows that at the V and VIII grades near about 98 per cent of the students passed in the examination conducted by the schools. However, it is also observed that very few students could secure 60 per cent and above marks in these examination. The children who secure more than 60 per cent of marks are less than 50 per cent, in all the districts at both the levels. In addition it is also observed that success rates are lower for girls in comparison to boys at the primary level, but at the upper primary level success rate improved and disparity was narrow down. Lowest scored marks at the primary level both for the girls and boys are in Latitpur and Chitrakoot districts. Situation is slightly better at the upper primary level. Both 40 per cent of boys and girls scored more than 60 per cent marks, except Lalitpur district. Generally it is said that the schools with low female teachers have low girls enrolment and low performance. This is to a large extent true in case of Bundelkhand Region of U.P. In all the districts women teachers' percentage is less than 50 per cent at both the levels.

**Table 11.12: Pass Percentage at the Primary and Upper Primary Levels**

| | *Primary* | | | | *Upper Primary* | | | |
|---|---|---|---|---|---|---|---|---|
| | *Boys* | | *Girls* | | *Boys* | | *Girls* | |
| *Bundelkhand Districts* | *Passed* | *60 & above* | *Passed* | *60 & above* | *Passed* | *60 & above* | *Passed* | *60 & above* |
| Banda | 97.4 | 35.7 | 96.6 | 31.7 | 98.5 | 42.4 | 98.6 | 49.0 |
| Hamirpur | 98.2 | 47.8 | 98.1 | 42.2 | 97.4 | 46.3 | 98.3 | 46.9 |
| Jhansi | 97.1 | 46.0 | 96.7 | 45.0 | 96.7 | 38.5 | 96.3 | 41.6 |
| Mahoba | 98.3 | 37.2 | 98.4 | 35.2 | 97.6 | 43.7 | 98.7 | 50.6 |
| Lalitpur | 97.4 | 22.4 | 97.6 | 20.6 | 96.6 | 16.2 | 97.3 | 18.5 |
| Chitrakoot | 98.2 | 28.4 | 98.1 | 22.4 | 98.1 | 47.8 | 98.7 | 44.9 |
| Jalaun | 98.2 | 38.7 | 97.6 | 33.6 | 98.5 | 35.9 | 98.9 | 37.1 |

*Source*: DISE, NUEPA, 2006-07, New Delhi

## Challenges for Education in the Region

- The Bundelkhand Region of U.P. has been educationally backward as its literacy rate (48.41 per cent) and literacy among woman (34.98 per cent) confirm it. More than half the population of the region is without any literacy skills. All the districts of the region have low level of literacy rates. Female literacy which is considered to be more sensitive index of social development is almost one third (34.98 per cent) of the region. Lalitpur district has lowest female literacy rate among all the districts, near about three forth per cent of people in the district are without literacy skills.
- In the region migration of economically poor population is another factor behind the non-enrolment of their children. As the region is backward, education is not a priority for the people. The infertile land and the rain fed agricultural economy based on it are unable to meet the basic requirement (food and shelter) of its population. Economic backwardness and low industrial growth rate leaves the poor population without work for most of the period in a year. In order to earn their livelihood they always move from one place to another. For the children of migratory population providing education is a challenging task for the government.
- Disparity exists because of physical infrastructure on account of difficult terrain and ecological conditions. In India according to norm, schools are opened on the basis of number of villages, not habitations or hamlets. The district plans shows that because

of the topography of the region every hamlet doesn't cover schools. The variations in provision of schools within the easy reach of children are a major challenge in rural and remote areas. Opening of small schools in every hamlet is not viable financially and academically.

- In the region educational facilities are expanded rapidly. The interventions by SSA helped in opening more numbers of schools in the region. Data shows that even then large numbers of children are still out of schools, especially of the age group 11-14. At upper primary level, out of 7 districts of the region in 3 districts GRE is less than 20 per cent. At the primary level though GER is 100 per cent in 6 districts, but it contains overage children. Therefore specific strategies for planned development are still needed, as more than half of the population is illiterate.
- In remote villages' free supply of text books, and other material hardly reach to them in time. Because of unavailability of text books it becomes difficult for the children to continue their schooling in future. In addition DISE data shows that basic facilities like drinking water, toilets especially for girls are another major cause for the children not to attend the schools. In one of the meeting, it was mentioned that poverty alone is not the factor interfering education of girls, even the feudal lords or well off families do not like their daughters to continue studies after primary education. They think that this much of education is sufficient for them.
- Shortage of female teachers is another challenge for the region. Research evidences tells that the schools with low female teachers have low girls enrolment and these schools performed low. This is to a large extent true in case of Bundelkhand Region of U.P. The participation of girls is less than 40 per cent (Table 11.7) and records say there is lesser number of women teachers. In all the districts women teachers' percentage is less than 50 per cent at both the levels primary as well as upper primary (Table 11.10). Parents in rural areas don't like their daughters to be taught by male teachers. Availability of less number of female teachers is one of the reasons for low enrolment of girls in primary and upper primary schools. As enough girls are not educated, there is less availability of female teachers. The vicious circle is going on since decades. It is very essential to break this circle to bring gender equality. Therefore to improve the girls participation in the region recruitment of female teachers is required.

- The region has difficult topography, lowest electrification of villages and lowest road connectivity. Because of lowest road connectivity the transport services are not regular, quick and timely. In one of the meeting an official from Lalitpur district mention that most of the teachers travel by bus to reach to their schools. Because of the less road connectivity and irregular bus service, it is difficult for teachers to reach in time the schools. Most of the time they close school also early then fixed time to catch bus.
- It is very essential that the provisions that are created for the disadvantaged sections of the population reach to them. The state government had provided financial incentives for education of girls and children from disadvantaged children and tried to increase access, enrolment and retention of these children. The records show that still large numbers of children are not getting the benefit of education. They are out of school. It is therefore essential to rethink planning approaches in context of topography of Bundelkhand region, so that disparities and inequity among the population can be removed and all the children of the age group 6-14 come in the purview of education. The starting point is diagnosing the situation or current disparities. Accordingly specific targets need to be set for particularly marginalized sections and un-served areas. Effective monitoring tools need to be devised for proper implementation of the strategies. So that progress towards the equity targets could be monitored from time to time.
- An adequate supply of motivated, qualified and properly trained teachers is a foundation of good-quality education. Recruitment of para-teachers helps in reaching marginalized groups and un-served areas, but state government has to look into consequences of teacher quality. Looking at the data (Table 11.11), pass percentage with good grades at the V class and VIII class is found very less for both boys and girls. In addition Gross Enrolment Ratio at the upper primary level is less than 50 per cent (Table 11.6) and out of them also less than 50 per cent students are securing good marks (60 per cent and above). Given that elementary education is a minimum need of the people in the present world, the data shows that to provide quality education efforts are required. The government can provide incentives for qualified and trained teachers to locate in un-served areas and provisions to increase recruitment from disadvantaged communities.

- Uneducated and poor parents relate education with employment. An official from Uttar Pradesh reported that the attitude of parents towards education is also one of major cause of low enrolment of children in the schools. They often say, what is the use of education to children? Are they going to get job after some education? Or they are going to lose their time in schooling? These are the questions frequently asked by the people in the region. Parents prefer to send their children to generate some money in various activities, rather them to send them to schools.

**Government's Initiatives for Achieving the Goals of UEE**

*Expanding Access:* In order to make schools accessible and within the reach of children, the State revised the previous norms for opening of the schools and reduced the distance to 1 km for primary and 3 km for upper primary schools to be opened.

*Village Education Committee (VECs)*: VECs were constituted in each village. One of their functions is to bring positive attitudinal change in people towards education and mobilize the community and motivate parents/ guardians to send their children to schools, especially girls and children from disadvantaged groups. They were also made responsible for school construction and maintenance, purchase of materials, school mapping and micro-planning exercise, preparation of Village Education Plan and school management as well as monitoring the performance of teachers.

*Promoting Girls' Education:* For promoting girls' education many initiatives were taken in the Bundelkhand region. At the primary school level these initiatives are; enrolment drive, Meena Campaign, 'Ma beti mela', 'Kishori sangh', Orientation and training camps for Village Education Committee members and Block Resource Coordinators and Cluster resource Coordinators. Summer camps to bring out of school girls in school, and providing bridge courses or condense courses for out of school children, and remedial coaching for weaker girls.

At the upper primary level initiative has been started in 'Meena Manch' to promote the confidence of girls and give them life skill education. These Manchs have a range of art and craft activities for skill development like stitching, making soft toys etc., which would help them in generating income as well. These life skill camps also familiarize the adolescents with issues related to family, health care, including reproductive health; safe motherhood, AIDS etc. In addition Child Care Centers to relieve girls from sibling care have been opened. The schools also distribute free uniforms to girls. Libraries have been set up in these schools in collaboration with National Book Trust. Another innovative step Kasturba Gandhi Balika Vidhalaya (KGBV) Scheme launched in 2004 aims to deal with issues relating to gender gaps, regular attendance of girls and transition to upper primary stage. This initiative seems to be very effective as girls who could not be sent to formal schools in the same village due to socio-economic reasons; their parents now willingly send their girls to KGVBs.

*Education Guarantee Scheme:* Under the Education Guarantee Scheme (EGS) primary schools were opened for class 1 and 2 in habitations, with no primary school within a radius of 1 km and 30 children in the age group of 6 to 11 yrs.

*Mid-Day Meal:* For increasing the enrolment the State Government launched cooked mid-day meal programme for nourishment of children in primary and upper primary schools.

**Education of Children with Special Needs (CWSN)**

The National commitment of providing free education to all children of the age group of 6-14 years will remain a distant dream unless children with special needs are included into the umbrella of education. Estimates indicate that 5-10 per cent of children in the State either do not enrol in primary school or dropout due to a variety of physical or learning related disabilities.

To enrol children with special needs in primary school or they do not drop out from the school, many initiatives have been taken by the government. Early detection and integration of such children, medical and functional assessment, supply of aids and appliances, special-teacher training programmes etc are conducted in collaboration with various NGOs and Handicapped Welfare Department.

**Quality Improvement**

The teacher pupil ratio has a significant bearing on quality of education. To bring the teacher pupil ratio to the national norm i.e. 40:1, para- teachers were recruited for the primary schools in the region.

**Teacher Training Programme**

Empowerment and capacity building of teachers lie at the core of all the quality programmes. Teachers are regularly given various in-service and refresher course trainings focusing various pedagogical areas. The modules developed for the purpose are: 1. 'Shikshakodaya' module focusing on motivating the teachers and improving their self image; 2. 'Sabal' emphasizing on developing the content knowledge of primary teachers and equipping them to use the new textbooks for Maths (class 2-3) in the classroom effectively; 3. 'Saadhan' on effective use of textbooks in the classroom, up gradation of content knowledge of teachers, use of new transitional methodologies, handling multi-grade and multi-level teaching and preparation of content specific teaching learning materials; 4. 'Samridhha' focusing Block and Cluster Resource coordinators to carry out their responsibilities effectively at upper primary level; 5. 'Sankalp' comprehensively talks about the leadership qualities and roles and responsibilities of head master as the leader of the school; 6. 'Effective School Library' focusing on how to inculcate reading habits among children through school library; and 7. 'Pathan Kshamta Vikas' to make teachers oriented towards techniques of reading skill-pronunciation, modulation.

### Textbooks and Teacher Guides

Child friendly textbooks developed both for primary and upper primary grades are being used. Teacher guides based on these new textbooks have also been prepared to reinforce the child centered pedagogy.

### Conclusion

In spite of various initiatives taken by the government to achieve the goal of UEE in Bundelkhand region of U.P. vast disparities were observed in terms of literacy, access, participation, and gender. These disparities threaten to undermine efforts to achieve universalization of elementary education in the region. Time has come now to make a clear shift in focus towards addressing the other more critical parameters such as retention/ dropout, attendance, transition and learning levels. There is need to widen and deepen the range of investigations to include empirical studies, analysis of available data, assessment of impact of programme interventions and factors influencing the achievement of UEE.

## REFERENCE

Ahluwalia, Montek S. (2002), "State Level Performance under Economic Reforms in India", in *Economic Policy Reforms and the Indian Economy*, ed. by Anne O. Krueger, Oxford University Press, New Delhi, pp. 91-125.

Alvesson, M. and Billing, Y.D., (1997), Understanding Gender and oOganisations, Sage publications, London.

Bala Nidhi and Bora Suniti Rani, Universalisation of Elementary Education in Uttar Pradesh, www.aiaer.net

Bhattacharya B. B. and Sakthivel, (2003), Regional Growth and Disparity in India: A Comparison of Pre and Post-Reform Decades, Discussion Paper, www.emeraldinsight.com

Census of India 2001, Series 1, *India, Provisional Population Totals*, Paper 1 of 2001. Delhi: Controller of Publications, Registrar General & Census Commissioner, India 2001

Chakraborty Sudip, (2006). Demand side Factors of children's school participation: An exploration with household survey data for rural North Bengal, *Journal of Educational planning and Administration,* Vol. XX, No. 2, April 2006, pp. 189-204.

Colclough, Christopher and Keith M. Levin (1993). *Educating All Children: Strategies for Primary Schooling in the South,* Clarendon, Oxford

National University of Educational Planning and Administration, New Delhi, (2008), District Information System for Education, 2006-07.

Dolan Sabine, (2005), Empowering Girls through Education in India, New York, www.unicef.org

Dreze J. and Gazdar H., Uttar Pradesh: The Burden of Inertia, in: Dreze J. and Sen A.K. (ed) *Indian Development: Selected Regional Perspectives,* Delhi: Oxford University Press, 1997.

Government of India (2005a), *Report of the CABE Committee on Free and Compulsory Education Bill and Other Issues Related to Elementary Education,* June 2005. Available at www.education.nic

Govinda R (2006) Literacy and Elementary Education in India: Regional Imbalances and Social Inequities. Paper presented at National Seminar on Education Commission at India Habitat Centre, New Delhi, December 26-28, 2006, organized by NUEPA.

Govinda R and Biswal K (2006) Elementary Education in India: Promises, Performance and Prospects, A Background Paper for Mid-Term Assessment of Tenth Plan, HDRC, UNDP, India

Govinda R and Biswal K (2007) Access to Elementary Education in India: Identifying Issues, Gaps and Priorities, CREATE-NUEPA, New Delhi, mimeo

Govinda R, P. Geetha Rani and Biswal, K. (2007) Progress in Elementary Education across States in India, CREATE-NUEPA, New Delhi, mimeo

*Government of India, Plan Documents from First to Tenth Five-Year Plans,* Planning Commission, !950-2007, New Delhi.

Jhingran D. (2003) Universalisation of Elementary Education, Government Policies.

Kulkarni P.M. (2002), Inter-State Variations in Human Development Differentials among Social Groups in India, *Working Paper Series No. 80,* National Council for Allied Economic Research

Mcdougall Lori (2000) Gender Gap in Literacy in Uttar Pradesh ; Questions for Decentralized Educational Planning, *Economic and Political Weekly* May 6, 2000.

MHRD (2000), *Sarva Shiksha Abhiyan A Programme for Universal Elementary Education; Framework for Implementation,* Ministry of Human Resources Development, Government of India, New Delhi.

National Policy on Education, 1986, MHRD, New Delhi.

Nagaraj, R, Aristomene Varoudakis and Marie-Ange Veganzones (1998), "Long-Run Growth Trends and Convergence across Indian States", OECD Technical Papers, No.131, January, pp. 1-58.

Nayar Usha, (1994). Universal Primary Education of Rural Girls in India, NCERT, New Delhi.

Nayar Usha, (2004). Situational Analysis of Women in the State of Uttar Pradesh (Ed.), National Commission for Women, New Delhi

Pai, Sudha (2005). 'Universal Elementary Education in India: An exploratory study of movements in civil society' in Ashok Swain (ed.) *Education and social action: Knowledge, identity and power*, UNRISD and Palgrave,

Programme of Action, 1992, MHRD, New Delhi.

Public Report on Basic Education (PROBE), 1996, New Delhi: OUP.

Ramchandran Vimla (1998), The Indian experience, in bridging the gap between intention and action- girls and women's education in South Asia: UNESCO-PROAP and ASPBAE, Bangkok and New Delhi.

Rao, M. Govinda, R.T. Shand and K.P. Kalirajan (1999), "Convergence of Incomes Across Indian States – A Divergent View", *Economic and Political Weekly*, March 27,

Sen A., 1997, Radical needs and modern reforms, in J. Dreze and A.K.Sen.

Shand, Ric and S. Bhide (2000), "Sources of Economic Growth – Regional Dimensions of Reforms", *Economic and Political Weekly*, October 14, pp. 3747-3757.

Tilak, J.B.G. (1996). 'How Free is Free Primary Education in India?', *Economic and Political Weekly,* vol.31 (4 & 5), pp.275-282; 355-366.

Singh Ajit Kumar, (2006). *Uttar Pradesh Development Report, 2000*, New Royal Book Co., Lucknow.

Tilak, Jandhyala B. G. (2004). 'Free and compulsory education: Legislative intervention', *Economic and Political Weekly*, February 14, 2004

Thukral Enakshi Ganguly, Poverty and Gender in India: Issues and Concern-Defining an agenda for poverty, proceedings of the First Asia and pacific Forum on Poverty (Vol. 1)

Uttar Pradesh brief profile: State development scenario, North India Human Development Report- National Council for Applied Economic Research

Victoria A. Velkoff, (1998), Women of the World, Women's Education in India, International Programme Centre, US Department of Commerce, Economics and Statistics Administration, Bureau of the Census.

Vina Mazumdar, (1989) Gender Issues and Education Development in Asia, CWDS, New Delhi.

World Bank, (1997a), India: Achievement and Challenges in Reducing Poverty, Washington, DC.

World Bank, (2003). A Review of Educational Progress and Reform In The District Primary Education Program, Human Development Sector, South Asia Region.

Zaidi S.M.I.A. (2005). Provision and Utilization of Elementary Education Facilities in North East India: What DISE Data Reveal? *New Frontiers in Education.* Vol. XXXV (3).

# 12

# Child Rights and Educational Access

***Prabuddh Kumar Mishra and Mary Bini. A***

*Children* and *childhood* across the world, have broadly been construed in terms of a 'golden age' that is synonymous with innocence, freedom, joy, play and the like. It is the time when, spared the rigours of adult life, one hardly shoulders any kind of responsibility or obligations. But, then, it is also true that children are vulnerable, especially when very young. The fact that children are vulnerable, they need to be cared for and protected from 'the harshness of the world outside' and around (Holt, 1975). Socially and physically speaking children represents the weakest pall of society. As children are vulnerable and don't have political voice, it is the responsibility of the society to give them equal opportunity in all sphere of life either in terms of Right to Education (RTE) or right to life. In this context protection of children has been ensured from time to time by international agencies in general and state in particular through the introduction of child rights in different spheres. Human relations in modern world are best way communicated and understood in the language of rights. United Nation Organization adopted the Universal Declaration of Human Rights on 10th December 1948. Since then, the notion of rights started percolating into every domain of human activity. Thus, we speak the language of rights in perceiving and in having perspective on social reality. The history of rights began with 'individual', and traversed through classes and masses; caste and creed; gender and nations; religion and region and finally reach to the children. Thus we have special convention and rights for children which guarantee many rights starting from right to love and name to nationality. Indian context, out of these rights, Right to Education (RTE) is considered one of the mile stones in the history of child rights.

## Child Rights: Indian Constitution

Indian leadership, at the dawn of independence, in the spirit of history of rights, guaranteed fundamental rights to its entire citizen. Apart from these enforceable rights, RTE Article 45, to all children was incorporated in the Directive Principle of State Policy which is not an enforceable right. To facilitate the government to implement the non-enforceable right effectively Indian Constitution spelt out no compulsory work for children in Article 23 and abolished child labour in hazardous industries through Article 24. Further, Constitution of India equipped the Legislature with Article 15 (3) to make separate legislations in the best interests of children. When all these constitutional provisions failed to yield desired results, to make RTE an enforceable right at par with Fundamental Rights, in the light of Supreme Court judgement, Indian parliament through a Constitutional amendment passed "The Right of Children to Free and Compulsory Education-2009". Educational processes are now being understood and evaluated from the perspective of Child Rights. Thus, it is generally believed, and continued to believe that schooling facilities every child, who attends it, to enjoy guaranteed rights equally. But educational reality says a different story. Educational reality, along with and apart from all other inequalities, is suffering from educational access inequality in the form of class, gender etc. Therefore there is need to evaluate guaranteed rights and thereby emanating policies and practices in the light of Constitutional values enshrined in its Preamble. The expression of child rights is unique. Normally a child is considered as a person not more than 12 years of age. However in terms of education it has been recognised to be not less than 6 years and not more than 14 years. The Juvenile Justice Act, 1986 however recognises the age for children in conflict with law as up to 18 years. Obviously the Legislature in its wisdom has adopted different age groups of children depending upon the nature of the protection perceived as required. As such Indian Law recognises these rights for children from conception (subject to being born alive) to the age of 18 years when a person becomes legally adult. The expression of child rights is therefore covered by different legislations in our country. The Constitution of India empowers the State to make special provisions for children; clauses (e) and (f) of article 39 provide that the state shall direct its policy towards securing that the tender age of children is not abused. The framers of the Constitution have exhibited sensitive approach to secure and safeguard the interest and welfare of children. Article 21A has now made education as a fundamental right for all children in the age group of six to fourteen.

National Policy for the welfare of children proclaims "The nation's children are supremely important asset...equal opportunities for development to all children during the period of growth should be our aim, for this would serve our large purpose of reducing inequality and ensuring social justice." National Policy on Education, 1986 also recognises children as precious national asset and an investment for the future.

**Landmarks in Rights to Children**

| | |
|---|---|
| (1) 1920: | The first Charter of Rights of the Child created (league of Nations adopted Charter of the Rights of child) |
| (2) 1959: | United Nation General Assembly (UNGA) Declaration of Right to the Child |
| (3) 1960-66: | UNESCO held 4 world conferences on Education |
| (4) 1979: | International Year for Children |
| (5) 1989: | Convention on the Right of Child |
| (6) 1990: | International Year for Girl Child |
| (7) 1990: | World Summit for Children |

Among these concerted efforts, special mention may be made to 1989's Convention on the Right of Child as it deals with all possible dimensions of children's rights. India signing on to it in 1991, we saw the introduction of a rights-based framework to educational access and children's participation in education. This historic convention has three parts with 54 articles. Among them, Article 28 deals with Right to Education, and Article 31 deals with right to rest, leisure and play recreation etc. The 1959, UNGA Declaration of Right to the Child is based on the principle that "*mankind owes to the child the best it has to give*". Implicit in this premise is an emphasis on duties towards the children and hence children's rights in the sense of claims. Its preamble refers to rights and freedoms. The ten principles set out in this do not embrace children's liberties at all. The declaration thus became a proclamation of general principles. A child is stated to have a right to:

- Affection, love and understanding
- Become useful member of the society and to develop their special talents
- Have enough time and space to play
- Have a name and nationality
- Be rescued first if any disaster takes place
- Proper housing, enough food and medical care
- Free education
- Special care if they are handicapped
- Grow up believing in peace and treating all people as their brother and sisters.

The Right to Education is high on the agenda of the international community. It is affirmed in numerous human rights treaties and recognized by governments as pivotal in the pursuit of development and social transformation. This recognition is exemplified in the international goals, strategies and targets that have been set during the past 20 years. The Education for All goals were established at Jomtien (Thailand) in 1990 and reaffirmed at the 2000 World Education Forum in Dakar (Senegal). In the Millennium Development Goals, established in 2000, the world's governments committed to achieve universal access to free, quality and compulsory primary education by 2015. In 'A World Fit for Children', the outcome document from the United Nations General Assembly Special Session on Children in 2002, governments reaffirmed these commitments and agreed to a range of strategies and actions to achieve them. More ambitious targets have been established in many regions. Countries in Latin America and the Caribbean, for example, are increasingly making school attendance compulsory for children of pre primary age. These various strategies have had an effect: In 1948, when education was recognized as a human right, only a minority of the world's children had access to any formal education; now a majority of them go to school, and participation in formal education beyond the elementary stages has increased.

Focusing on the goal of human rights-based approach to education is simple: to assure every child a quality education that respects and promotes her or his right to dignity and optimum development. Achieving this goal is, however, enormously more complex. Child right especially RTE is high on the agenda of the international community. It is affirmed in numerous human rights treaties and recognized by governments as pivotal in the pursuit of development and social transformation. India made a Constitutional commitment to provide free and compulsory education to all children up to the age of 14, nearly sixty years ago. The goal, which was expected to be achieved by 1960, remains elusive, even now. Yet, one has to admit that developments in recent years have had significant impacts on the situation, raising the hope that universal basic education could be a reality within a reasonable period of time.

## Right to Education Act: Conceptual Issues

From RTE movement started in 1988 to Supreme Court judgment in 1993, our politicians took twenty one long years to give education as a fundamental right to the children of India. Even though nearly all educationally developed countries attained their current educational status by legislating free and compulsory education – Britain did so in 1870 – India has dithered and lagged behind in introducing such legislation, with grave consequences. Of the nearly 200 million children in the 6 to 14 age group, more than half do not complete eight years of elementary education, as never enrolled or dropouts. Of those who do complete eight years of schooling, the achievement levels of a large percentage, in language and mathematics, is unacceptably low. It is no wonder that a majority of the excluded and non-achievers come from the most deprived sections of society – Dalits, OBCs, Adivasis, girls, Muslims and poor– precisely the people who are supposed to be empowered through education (Rana, 2009).

Thus it has taken 55 years from Independence to make education a fundamental right of children and a further 6 years for the Right to Education Bill to be introduced in Parliament (APF, 2009).

RTE fails to follow UN's Child Rights Convention "the Act needs to bring into its ambit all children in the age group of 3-16 years. It ignores children who are below 6 years of age" (Azim Premji Foundation, 2009). With heightened political consciousness amongst the deprived and marginalized, never in the history of India has the demand for inclusive education been as fervent as today. Yet even a cursory examination of the proposed Act shows some glaring shortcomings, like the age of the child. As a signatory to the UN Child Rights Convention, India has accepted the international definition of a child, which is up to age 18. The Act covers only children from age 6 to 14, clearly excluding and violating the rights of the 0-6 and 14 to 18 year olds. This problem can be traced to the 86th amendment and its article 21A, which defines the age from 6 to 14. As an Act flowing out of the amendment, it is clear that it cannot go beyond Article 21A, which makes it imperative that the 86th amendment must be re-amended to correct this anomaly, and once that happens, the change needs to be reflected in the corresponding act at that point of time. Having made education fundamental right it needs to be recognised that the challenge of elementary education is to somehow find a way to deal with the elusive triangle of access, equity and quality. In this context educational access in India has a poor face at par with UN standards.

The basic aspect of *educational access* is the provision of a school in the proximity of a child, since there are still areas in the country where such access is lacking. The Act envisages that each child must have access to a neighbourhood school within three years from its enactment. The presence of a nearby school is, however, no guarantee that a child can indeed access it. One of the key barriers, particularly for the poor and the deprived, is the issue of cost. That is where one of the critical aspects of Article 21A comes into play, namely, the State shall provide 'free' education. Normally, 'free' is interpreted as non payment of fees by the parents of the child. But numerous studies have concluded that the fee constitutes only one of the components of educational expenditure. And since the landless, poor and socially deprived cannot meet the other expenses, this result in the non-participation of their children in education.

These other expenses differ from place to place, though uniforms, copies and books and so on are perhaps common. The Act defines free education to mean any fee, expense or expenditure that keeps a child from participating in education, and obliges the State to provide all these. This broader definition, with implications for higher expenditure by the State, appears to be a better way to meet the challenge of access in terms of costs, rather than providing a list of items that will be covered, which are difficult to anticipate in different locations and in the future and hence cannot be exhaustive (Sadgopal, 2009; Rana, 2009).

Sustained participation in schooling is, however, equally influenced by the *quality of access*. The high non retention rates in spite of higher enrolments in recent years are a clear indication that concerns of quality cannot be postponed till access is guaranteed, as also by the increasing tendency to seek out questionable private schools perceiving their quality to be 'better'. The approach of providing schooling through education guarantee centers and untrained para teachers has also greatly exacerbated the problem of quality of government schools ever since the District Primary Education Programme pioneered this cost-cutting strategy, further expanded through the Sarva Shiksha Abhiyan (SSA) in many states of the country. This approach has resulted in making education more iniquitous, since the government system itself now has a variety of streams – the EGS centre, the rundown rural or *basti* school, the alternative school, the Kendriya, Sarvodaya, Navodaya and other kinds of schools and so on (Sadgopal, 2009).

Clearly, access to each is determined according to the social and class background of children, thus segregating them further. Consequently, the social integration that education was expected to assist, by bringing children from diverse backgrounds together in the same classrooms, has been allowed instead, one may say deliberately, to experience higher degrees of fragmentation. No wonder then that an increasing number of parents, both urban and rural, despite great financial difficulties, are attracted to the option of purchasing education from private profit-making schools that seem to have external frills of quality and regular presence of teachers.

If one focuses on the guarantee of quality of education under RTE, while ensuring that every child who traverses through the elementary education system acquires a certificate of completion, the Act fails to guarantee that a child has acquired competencies deriving from said education process. No standards are set for learning outcomes. A case of guaranteeing graduation but not education. Failure of the child to attest to acquisition of competencies is also not flagged for remedial action and/or systemic enhancements. The Act should also define a framework to measure the quality of education imparted (APF, 2009).

In government schools, teachers have been frequently pulled out of schools for cross-checking voter lists and election training. Essentially no teaching will take place for a week around the polling date. The private school children of course do not suffer such loss of teaching. On the contrary, it will be legitimized since the Act provides for deployment of government teachers for "decennial census, election to Local Authorities, State Legislatures and Parliament and disaster relief duties." Government school children will continue to sacrifice their education to keep the Indian democracy alive, while the private school children will receive education undisturbed (Sadgopal, 2009).

Finally, the Bill is silent on the aspect of actual competence of and quality of monitoring by the national and state commissions for protection of child rights. While the provisions provide that an aggrieved person may lodge a complaint with the local authority, there is an obvious problem in this clause, since the very same body that is responsible for ensuring protection of the rights of the child is also made responsible for deciding upon a complaint against it. The bill is silent on the state parties that will be held responsible if its implementation is found lackadaisical.

## Educational Access

Provision of quality education in India is an enormous quantitative challenge. The data available from the Ministry of Human Resource Development (MHRD, 2004-2005) showed that 182 million students were enrolled in 1.04 million elementary schools (grades 1-8) across the country (GOI, 2007a). This accounted for approximately 82 per cent of children in the 5-14 year age group in that year (GOI, 2007b). Over the past two decades demand for schooling in India has increased, but provision is unequal. The National Policy on Education (NPE, 1986) and its Programme of Action (POA) (1992) state that all children, irrespective of caste, creed, location or gender, should have access to elementary education of a comparable quality. But in reality, schooling provision favours those better off, and disadvantaged groups (including poor children, girls, children from Scheduled Caste (SC), Scheduled Tribe (ST), Other Backward Class (OBC) groups have less access and access to poorer quality education. Large variations in access exist across different states, geographical areas, and social categories such as gender, caste and ethnicity. Policy makers whilst making great strides to improve physical access to schools, have ongoing challenges to provide meaningful access for all children in India.

## Patterns of Educational Access in India

Access to basic education in India is improving, but areas of concern remain:

*School Supply*

The number of primary schools has grown rapidly from 529, 000 in 1986 to 767, 000 in 2005 and at upper primary from 134, 000 to 275, 000. In 2003 around 87 per cent of habitations had a primary school within a distance of 1 km and 78 per cent of habitations had an upper primary school within 3 km (NCERT, 2005). In addition, the number of private pre-primary, primary and upper primary schools has also increased considerably. However, government and local bodies continue to be the main providers managing around 91 per cent of primary and 73 per cent of upper primary schools. Many new schools particularly those opened under the EGS/AIE scheme are small in size. Most are located in rural areas. Around 28 per cent of children are educated in primary schools with 50 students or fewer (DISE 2005-6). Questions of quality of provision persist with many schools having weak infrastructure and poor teaching and learning conditions.

*Initial Access to Education*

According to gross enrolment (GER) data available at the national level, India has achieved near universal enrolment in primary education in most areas. The average GER across all India was 108.5 per cent at the primary level and 70.5 per cent at the upper primary level in 2004-05. GERs at primary varied from less than 80 per cent (Chandigarh, Punjab, to more than 120 per cent (Chhattisgarh, Arunachal Pradesh), and at upper primary from less than 60 per cent (Uttar Pradesh, Jharkhand, Bihar) to over 100 per cent (Tamil Nadu, Himachal Pradesh). Patterns of access are gendered. In 2004-05 around 88 per cent of boys and 79 per cent of girls were attending school nationally (GOI, 2007b). The reality of girls' exclusion is further complicated by caste, religion, ethnicity and age. Girls from poor, SC, ST and Muslim communities tend to be much more disadvantaged than their male counterparts, and a larger proportion of girls than boys from these groups are denied access to schooling.

*Rural Schools*

Rural schools cater for the vast majority of students nationally (85 per cent of total enrolments in primary schools in 2005). Yet rural schools tend to have poorer resources such as school infrastructure, teaching materials, fewer teachers per school and higher dropout rates. Over 80 per cent of primary schools have three teachers or less.

*Out of School Children*

There has been a steady decline in the number of out-of-school children in India. Data reported in the CAR suggests that in 2001, about 44 million (or 28.5 per cent of the total child population) were out of school. By

2005 estimates varied from a low of about 7 million to a high of about 30 million. The differences in estimates arise from different methods of sampling and accounting for repetition, drop out and over age enrolment. Inter-state variations are quite vast. In the Census of India in 2001 reported that about 70 per cent of the total out-of-school children in India in the 6-10 year old age group were concentrated in Uttar Pradesh, Bihar, Madhya Pradesh, West Bengal and Rajasthan. According to the 61st Round National Sample Survey (2006): 35 per cent of 5-29 years old have never been to school; and around 28.5 per cent of children dropped out of primary school in 2004-05. Many children who have initial access to school, attend irregularly, learn little and repeat grades. These children are at risk of dropping out. Numbers of silently excluded children are substantial, but difficult to quantify, not least because there is no standardised achievement data across India.

*Unaccounted for Children*

While statistics and official programmes recognise large groups of children that might be excluded from education, a substantial number of children in India are unaccounted for and unregistered. These children may be migrants, street children or children living in unauthorised slums. Many of these children will not be accessing education.

*Transition Patterns*

Not all children who complete primary schooling enter the upper primary stage. Data collected on all-India basis under the District Information System in Education (DISE) for 2005-06 showed that: on average, 16 per cent of children who reach Grade 5 fail to make the move from primary to upper primary school. Similarly about 15 per cent of children who reach Grade 8 fail to make the move from upper primary to secondary schooling because of a lack of schooling facilities near their homes, the direct and indirect costs, and because they haven't reached appropriate attainment levels.

There are many interacting factors which contribute to exclusion from schooling. The Indian context is so diverse that social stratification, gender inequity, location and poverty vary greatly across States and communities and often interact. Together they can form a complex nexus of exclusion and it is important to understand relationships between factors.

## Conclusion

How much education does India need, and for what purpose? We can readily agree that universal good quality basic education is a requisite and moral requirement of all modern societies, for the sake of social equity, cultural values, and economic functionality (Schwartzman 2004:12).

Throughout this article the analysis of child right, education and educational access demonstrated how people are still excluded from receiving what they are entitled to as a human right; a life in dignity, freedom and equality. Education is one of those rights that enable the full realization of a person's potential and inclusion in society by enabling citizenship and growth. Negative gaps on its realization, however, are perceptible around the world. In India the situation is not different as many children and adults are excluded from having the substance of their right translated into reality. In order to understand the degree to which the right to education is attained, an analysis of different aspects of the India's RTE legislation is carried out in this article.

## REFERENCE

APF 2009. http://www.azimpremjifoundation.org/html/EducationReading-reports.htm

Chowdhry, N.K. 2009. *Indian Constitution and Education.* Shipra Publication, Delhi.

GOI 2007a. *Selected Educational Statistics*, 2004-2005. New Delhi: Ministry of Human Resource Development.

______GOI 2007b. *Annual Report, 2006-2007*. New Delhi: Ministry of Human Resource Development.

________ 1997. *Convention on the Rights of the Child – Country Report, India, February 1997,* New Delhi: DWCD, MHRD, GOI.

________ 1997. *Child Welfare and Development: The Historical Perspective – 1787 to 1997,* New Delhi: DWCD, MHRD, GOI.

________ 2000. *India Report on the World Summit for Children*, New Delhi: DWCD, MHRD, GOI.

________ 2001. *Convention on the Rights of the Child – India First Periodic Report 2001,* New Delhi: DWCD, MHRD, GOI.

________ 2005. *National Plan of Action for Children 2005*, New Delhi: DWCD, MHRD, GOI.

_______. 2005. *The India Country Report on Violence against Children,* New Delhi: DWCD, MHRD, GOI.

Himes, J.R. 1992. "The UN Convention on the Rights of the Child: More than a New Utopia", *Innocenti Essays* No. 5.

Holt, J. 1975. *Escape from Childhood*, Harmondsworth: Penguin Books (first published in 1974).

India Alliance for Child Rights. 2003. *India – Every Right for Every Child: 2003 Citizens Alternate Review and Report on India's Progress Towards CRC Realisation*, New Delhi: IACR.

Mohanty, J. 2008. *Modern Trends in Indian Education,* Deep& Deep Publication. New Delhi.

Mukhopadhyay, M and Parhar, M (ed.) 2007. *Education in India: Dynamics of Development.* Shipra Publication, Delhi.

National Curriculum Framework 2005. NCERT, New Delhi.

National Policy of Education 1986. Government of India, New Delhi.

Parth, J.S. 2009. The Right of Children to Free and Compulsory Education Bill, 2008, Suggestions from the Centre for Civil Society. http://www.ccsindia.org/. [Accessed on 10-Nov-2011]

Patil, V. T. 2001. *Human Rights, Third Millennium Mission.* Author Press, Delhi.

Planning Commission of India, website www.planningcommission.gov.in in particular the Five- Year Plans.

Rana, V. 2009. Right to Education. *Economic and Political Weekly*, July 23, 2009, India: Sameeksha Trust Publications.

Sadgopal, A. 2006. "Center's Move Places Education at Risk", *The Hindu*, September 26, New Delhi.

Sadgopal, A. 2008. "Education Bill: dismantling rights", *The Financial Express*, 9, Novermber, 2008.

Schwartzman, S. 2004. The Challenges of Education in Brazil. Brazil: Symposium Books, 2004, pp. 9-40.

Swaminathan, Mina (ed.). 1998. *The First Five Years – A Critical Perspective on Early Childhood Care and Education in India*, New Delhi: Sage Publications.

# 13

# Investigating the Role of Community Participation in Elementary Schools

## *Dang District, Gujarat*

***Priti Chaudhari***

Education policy makers all over the world have come to view community participation as an effective means of promoting elementary education, both in terms of quantity and quality. Further, community participation and empowerment in decision making has commonly been understood and propagated as an attempt to counteract centralized actions. It is assumed that community participation and empowerment has the potential to make a major health and living conditions as well as enriching their life styles. The literacy campaigns in different parts of India have also, though not uniformly in all cases, demonstrated the potential role that community member can play for their own betterment.

A community is a group of people, who live in a geographical area and have an interest in each other for the purpose of making a living; it is a form of social organization existing between the family and state. It is locus for social systems of a particular kind composed of interacting social institutions which meet the basic human needs, through the function of which people have developed a sense of belongingness and a potential ability to act together as an entity. Community, while in itself consists of several parts (there are communities existing within a community), is also a part of larger social system. It is a dynamic social unit which is subject to change of internal or external origin. Some of the important characteristics of community are: communities are close-knit entities, their customs are interrelated, these communities are complexes of sub-group relationship and there is discernible leadership within the community (Dhuma and Bhatnagar, 1980). Communities can be defined by characteristics that the member share, such as culture, language, tradition, law, geography, class and race. There are in fact several conceptual uses of the term community in social sciences. The Anthropological Survey of India in its ethnographic mapping of communities in India defines community not only in territorial but sociological terms. It is conceptually used "as in ethnography, which is marked by endogamy, occupation and perception". Zenter (1964) points out three aspects of communities. First, community is a group structure, whether formally or informally organized; in which members play roles which are integrated around goals associated with the problems from collective occupation and habitational space. Second, members of the community have some degree of collective identification with the occupied space members. Lastly, the communities have some degree of local autonomy and responsibility. Shaeffer (1992) argues, some communities are homogeneous while others are heterogeneous; and some united while others conflictive. Some communities are governed and managed by leaders chosen democratically who act relatively autonomously from other levels of government, and some are governed by leaders imposed from above and represent central authorities. The concept of community thus, has been changing as per the needs of development and administration where by the communities had been reduced to groups of beneficiaries, stake holders or target populations in the framework of their projects. Therefore the understanding of community is essential to identify the context in which it is to be analyzed. It must be observed, however, that the concept of community defined in terms of face-to-face interaction in a spatial-temporal context is nevertheless meaningful in village India. Perhaps, it is with reference to school in villages that one can speak of school-community relations as per the conventional paradigm. It is in this context that the debate on community participation in primary education becomes important and meaningful.

Community participation is not a new concept in India. In the early years after independence, it was viewed and promoted as a part of the liberation rhetoric. In Gandhi's scheme of education a school was an integral part of community. Therefore the question of community participation in school affairs was not to be a matter of debate and discourse. However, the post independence years witnessed an altogether different phenomenon on the ground. With the virtual govermentalisation of primary education, schools became totally alienated from the community they served. Then again community participation became a major agenda of discussion in the country in the mind 1980 when decentralization began to be recognized as an important component of the educational reform and change process. It was realized that responsibility should be devolved as far as possible upon the people involved in the actual task of schooling, in consultation with the parents of pupil whom they taught. The move however appears to have been prompted essentially by the utilitarian value of involving the community, which could possibly improve the deteriorating efficiency and effectiveness of the school system.

The National Policy of Education (1986) and its Programme of Action (1992) recommended not only promoting participation of community in elementary education but also a move towards empowering the local community to make major management decisions in this regard. The NPE and POA suggested decentralized management of education at all levels (district, sub-district and panchayat levels) and involvement of people in decision making process. It proposed adopting, the eleventh schedule of the constitution which provides, among other things, for entrusting with Panchayati Raj bodies, "education including primary education and secondary schools, teachers training and vocational education adult and non-formal education, literacy and cultural activities". The subsequent 72nd and 73rd constitutional amendment passed in both the houses of the parliament gave further fillip to the move towards decentralization and community empowerment in the management of education. It recommended the delegation of authority related to education, including primary and secondary schools, technical training and vocational education, adult education and non formal education, and spread of literacy and cultural activities to Panchayati Raj bodies (Article 243 G of the 11th schedule). The eighth plan document clearly enunciated that "in the process of development people must operate and government must cooperate". Thus community participation over the past decade has been appropriated by almost any group working for change, be it in agriculture, welfare or education. The government therefore emphasized on involvement of community through number of committees (B.G. Kher Committee 1953, Balwant Rai Mehta Committee 1957, Sadiq Ali Committee 1964, Bhandari Committee 1969, Bongirwar Committee 1971 and Ashok Mehta Committee 1978) and almost all the successive schemes and programmes like Bihar Education Programme, Lok Jumbish and Shiksha Karmi. It is a matter of grave concern, that despite strong policy directives the community's role remained peripheral. In order to address this issue, the government launched in 1995 the DPEP in few educationally backward districts and through its experience in 2000 the 'SSA' in the entire nation that once again called for community ownership of schools through decentralized participatory approach. These programmes have the promotion of community participation as a major thrust area in their activities; they have tried to evolve special strategies for bringing community and school closer, and also to involve community members in a significant manner for development of primary education.

Community participation is one of the major strengths of SSA. Community Participation is interwoven in planning, implementation and monitoring of educational activities and hence, it is not to be viewed as a separate component. Participation of community by way of involvement of Panchayati Raj Institutions, voluntary organizations, local level cultural and social organizations, Non-Governmental Organizations, parents and individuals is crucial to the success of educational programmes, especially at the elementary stage of education. The underlying rationale is that education must have local support and community ownership in order to meet the educational needs of the children from the community. Strategies envisage a central role for the local community by way of involving the Panchayati Raj Institutions and the VEC in opening new schools, establishing non-formal education centers, holding literacy classes, identifying workforce from within community, providing land and buildings for educational programmes and indeed accepting overall responsibility related to all aspects of educational development, namely, planning, implementation, management, monitoring and evaluation.

Specifically, a variety of informal and formal structures have come in to existence such as Mother Teacher Associations under the DPEP, core team and women's group under Lok Jumbish in Rajastahn, apart from Village Education Committees and Parent Teacher Association in many states. Community participation and empowerment for primary education is gradually acquiring a place of importance not only in education but also in public administration.

Alongside these developments at policy level, the country has also witnessed major programmes of primary education in different states, particularly during the last decade. These programmes also have the promotion of community participation as a major thrust area in their activities: some of them have tried to evolve special strategies for bringing community and school closer and also to involve community members in a significant manner for elementary education development.

**Programmes having Community Participation as Thrust Area**

Many educational innovations of the recent years are based on the strong foundation of community support and participation. When progress is discussed and analyzed at different levels within the project, "people's acceptance and participation" is used as an indicator, mobilizing the village community to take responsibility to ensure quality education for every child was the core strategy for both Lok Jumbish (LJ) and Shiksha Karmi Project (SKP) in their efforts to universalize primary education and deliver quality education. It would not be far removed from truth if we say that community involvement has been the key factor for the success of the two projects.

LJ has had a positive impact on the empowerment of locally elected people, especially on female representatives at village level, who are often active members of the LJ core teams or women's groups. The village education committees carefully formed and trained through environmental building activities in the LJ programme are actively involved in school matters.

SKP has constituted Village Education Committee (VECs) in 2000 villages to promote community involvement in primary education and encourage village level planning. The role of the VEC as defined by SKP was to mobilize resources for maintenance, repair and construction of school infrastructure and also in determining the school calendar and school timings in consultation with the local community and Shiksha Karmis (educational workers).

The positive impact of the LJ and SKP was focusing on supporting the teachers and the students by involving, the village community in taking responsibility for all educational activities of the village school, in serving as a demonstration of how deeply rooted problems of education in India can be addressed.

The Mahila Samkhya Programme (MSP) was designed to mobilize the organize women for education through creating an environment for learning. MSP was being implemented in seven states in the country (Uttar Pradesh, Andhra Pradesh, Gujarat, Karnataka, Bihar, Madhya Pradesh and Assam) and covered over 5000 villages, had been recognized as an effective and successful mobilization strategy. The diverse impact of this learning process is discernible in all the MSP states. Women were addressing issues of access and improvement of civic amenities, problems of drinking water, wages, housing, ensuring education for girls, making schools and the health system more accountable, bravely confronting violence against women and social practices like child marriage and the devadasi system, confidently interacting and negotiating with power structures and are effectively participating in Panchayati Raj Institutions. While the direct impact of the MSP educational strategy is yet to be fully felt, its impact is most visible in the confidence with which 'Sanghas' are taking an active role in Village Education Committees, making schools work, ensuring that the teachers come regularly and in many instances, ensuring that in their villages, children, particularly girl children, have access to formal education.

In SSA, the community is expected to play a key role in micro-planning, especially in the development of Village/Ward Education Plan and School Improvement Plans. Community based monitoring in specific issues like enrolment, retention, education of girl child and other disadvantaged groups, utilization of various grants and construction of school building is important to ensure attainment of the programme objectives.

The following steps and activities were considered for involving the community at grassroots level:

*Empowerment of community*: The first step towards involving the local community is to build the capacity of community based institutions. Education has already been decentralized to panchayat level. SSA envisages constitution of local committees like the Village Education Committee, School Management Committee, Mother Teacher Association, Parent Teacher Association, and Village Civil Works Committee to look after educational issues. Appropriate capacity building measures for these institutions would go a long way in empowering the community to effectively discharge their statutory and community responsibilities towards schools and education in general.

*Generate community awareness towards education*: A variety of activities such as enrolment drive, awareness generation, children fair, participation in community fair, cultural program etc. had taken up under SSA. Campaigns and mobilization initiatives were organized focusing on specific issues like enrolment, retention, education of girl child and other disadvantaged group. Campaign to mobilize the special groups like girl child (mothers also), SC/ST/other backward classes, tribal and other disadvantaged groups to ensure their participation in the primary schools or alternative centers, were organized. Along with these campaigns, specific activities like meena campaign, maa-beti mela, mahila sanmelan, kishori mela, shishu mela, prabhat pheri etc. were conducted to ensure increased enrolment and reduce drop out.

*Involvement of community in micro level planning*: SSA envisages involvement of VEC and other community level organizations in habitation level planning and micro-planning exercises. Such involvement will further ensure their participation in the formulation of village education plan and school improvement plans. A core planning team had ideally be constituted in each village at the habitation level, including VECs, selected community leaders, NGO representatives, headmasters, teachers, parents, women, SC/ST/MTA/PTA/SMC representatives etc. Data generated through household survey should be the basis of such habitation level planning. The VECs/SMCs also has a significant role in the preparation and regular updating of the village education registers.

*Involvement of community in monitoring and supervision*: SSA provides a major role of the community in monitoring and supervision of school and other educational facilities. The community should ensure that all children come to school regularly and receive quality education. In many states the local community and panchayat has been empowered to recruit local level teachers, sanction teacher's leaves, decide on school timings and arrange for school infrastructure. Alternative schooling centers are mostly set up and managed by the local community. VECs/WECs along with the panchayat level monitoring committees can also monitor all the activities of school including academic activities. PTAs meeting can be held to discuss the progress of children. Help of PTAs can also be sought in preparation of TLM. VECs can also be trained to manage schools and monitor indicators like access, enrolment and retention.

*Construction and maintenance of school infrastructure*: Under SSA, it is also mandatory for involving the community in construction and maintenance of school infrastructure. All civil work funds under the programme are routed through the community. The VEC or a sub-committee is entrusted with all aspects of construction, including arranging for materials, keeping accounts and ensuring quality. The maintenance and repair grant of schools is also passed on to the VEC. The VEC is also entrusted with school improvement grant. This empowerment, in physical and financial terms, is expected to increase the stake of the community in the school building. The programmes also encourage community contribution in the construction of the school infrastructure, both financial as well as labour.

For the community to perform all the above roles, their capacity needs to be substantially improved. The community bodies viz. VEC/SMC/ Panchayat and community leaders need to be trained on their role in planning and monitoring. The various aspects of quality education also need to be explained to the local community in a simple way. As they are involved in construction, the community would also need to be trained on various technical aspects of construction. It is also important to train the community on various managerial and account keeping aspects.

Village Education Committee (VEC), Mother/Parents Teacher Associations (MTA/PTA) and Women Motivator Groups are the grass root level bodies which play a pivotal role in enlisting community participation for education and bringing the community and schools closer to establish an interactive and effective school management system. These bodies are expected to assume leadership to influence community thinking and guide their decisions in favour of their children, particularly girls. These organizations are also envisaged to motivate the spirit of community ownership of schools and the education system to the extent of mobilizing community resources for school improvement.

Involvement of functionaries, PTA/MTA and VEC members in school activities like schooling process of children, attending school events, attending meeting/ training, ensuring distribution of incentives, school mapping/ micro planning, stay arrangements for teachers, school planning and development had positive impact on improving elementary education (Sahoo, 2004). Therefore, unless the PRIs, local bodies, parents and community are involved in school activities, in all aspects of educational development, the goal of UEE will still remain a distant dream.

**Different Committees at grass root level**

(1) V*illage Education Committee (VEC) in villages and Ward Education committee (WEC) in municipal corporation*: VEC/WEC is constituted for the management of education at village level. The problems at the village level can be better understood by members of the village and they can think of some viable solution. Considering this factor VEC is constituted and is deputed with powers to carry on the management of school. This would generate interest amongst the community members and more and more people would get involved in promoting education. Thus VEC is established to universalize and ensure quality education at elementary level. It maintains village education register or ward education register, which keeps record of out of school children, irregular children and dropouts and then their responsibility will be given to the member of mother teacher association and parent teacher association. Concept behind this is teacher will teach and community will bring children to schools.

VEC—according to Gujarat Government Education Department Letter no. PRE/1295-1419 V (99) dated- 20/9/99 persons to be involved are given below.

1) Sarpanch
2) Cluster Resource Centre Coordinator
3) Talati
4) Two women from panchayat
5) School Head Master
6) Aganwadi Karyakar
7) Mid Day Meal Sanchalak
8) Retired Teacher
9) Secondary school Headmaster
10) Parents of disabled children (presently)
11) Parents of SC/ST children

*Functions*: The VEC or a sub-committee is entrusted with all aspects of

- Identifying needs of the schools.
- Conducting periodical meetings to ensure co-operation of the community, community mobilization.
- Assisting the headmaster in transparent utilization of grants released to schools and effective utilization of the funds.
- To manage the joint account of the VEC.

- Undertaking civil construction and maintenance works wherever assigned or needed.
- Enrolment of all school age children and ensuring cent per cent completion of elementary education of all children.
- Conducting campaigns and melas for UEE.
- Monitoring the academic performance of children, achievement levels, attendance and quality of education.
- Organizing functions and celebrations of school and public events, which showcase the skills of the students.
- Effective co-ordination of the community with implementing agencies.
- Displaying school data and receipts and expenditure of grants in the school public notice board.
- Involvement in teacher training.
- Involvement in appointment of educational volunteers for Education Guarantee Scheme and Alternative Innovative Education centers as per guidelines and direction.
- Monitoring the functioning of Education Guarantee Scheme and Alternative Innovative Education centers.

2. *Village Civil Works Committee* (*VCWC*): its main work is building repairing and Technical Resource Persons gives guidance to them

3. *Mother Teacher Association* (MTA) *and Parent Teacher Association* (*PTA*): To get maximum cooperation from parents and other members of the community in district primary education programmes MTA and PTA are constituted. The framework of SSA envisages that the constitution of different members in these committees be on democratic grounds providing opportunity to people from all sections of the society. It is constituted based on their participation, awareness and readiness to contribute services. A meeting of all parents is to be conducted and then from it a five member working committee of PTA and MTA is formed, amongst whom one will be the head, if the principal of the primary school is women, she becomes the head of MTA.

*Functions*: The functions of PTA and MTA are not different from VEC except that they do not have any financial power.

Thus SSA has very clearly demarcated the roles and responsibilities of each committee and empowered the members of community for effective supervision and monitoring. It has not only been one of the most comprehensive but also appropriate programmes for a country with such wide disparities. It has made maximum attempts to provide an opportunity for improving human capabilities to all children through provision of community owned quality education in mission mode.

## Responsibilities of Constituted School Committees under SSA

- Assessment of the educational needs of the village population through a process of micro-planning exercise every year.
- Maintaining micro level database for the children through a child register.
- Building of awareness of the community and mobilizing parents and community for ensuring enrolment and retention of children.
- Making recommendations/suggestions to the teacher for better performance of the school.
- To receive and utilize fund and maintain proper bank account. VEC/Ward Education Committee (WEC) is primarily responsible for sending utilization certificate of funds placed at its disposal to the higher authority. Fund which will be collected from the community/any person (donor) will be deposited in the same bank account and maintain expenditure statement separately.
- Identifying drop out children and ensuring their enrolment in different school set up.
- Arranging remedial teaching/alternative education, bridge course etc. by engaging community volunteers.
- Ensuring convergence of different rural/urban services (with the help of panchayat samiti/municipality) for building of school infrastructure/school beautification.
- Sending monthly report to CRC from VEC/WEC. Head teacher as secretary and panchayat member/council or as chairman of VEC/WEC will keep all records, reports etc. in their custody. VEC/WEC will maintain accounts; preserve all vouchers, cashbooks, reports etc. and place before the parents and community time to time for ensuring transparency.
- Establishing Education Guarantee Scheme/Alternative Inclusive Education in unserved habitations.
- Ensuring enrolment and retention of the children of SC/ST and minority groups, other categories of special focus group namely, hardest to reach children/ Deprived Urban children etc.
- Organizing parents meeting in the form of PTA/MTA on quarterly basis.

## Rationale of the Study

In order to enhance the standard of living of the people, their social and economic development is essential. This indicates that education must be relevant to the community. If this has to be done, then, community participation in the educational system will be necessary. It is more so at elementary level, where all learning has to be concretized more meaningfully with the help of work situations existing in immediate community and environment. Community participation is needed even to bring first generation learners to school. Even to ensure regular attendance of children in the school and guiding educational activities of children out of school will require community involvement. In order to maintain quality of school education at elementary level community involvement in school management and other activities appear to be inevitable.

Moreover, Enhancement of community participation in elementary education not only helps in improvement of primary education of tribal areas but also helps in achieving the goal of UEE. With this end in view, it is highly advisable to conduct research and experiment on tribal community participation in different aspects of elementary education in educational context.

In Gujarat, Dang is the only district having 98 per cent of tribal population. When DPEP was launched first time in Gujarat in selected three backward districts that require special attention under SSA based on six criteria, Dang is the only district that fall under three criteria viz. special focus districts (Ministry of Human Resource Development), Districts with ST population more than 50 per cent and special focus districts (Tribal Welfare Department), (Annual Work Plan and Budget Dang 2009-10). Dang is smallest district on southern fringes of Gujarat State, comprises mainly of a single rural hilly forested taluka at the edge of Sahyadries. The total area is 1, 778 Sq. Km. Ahwa is headquarter of the Dang district covering extreme length of 59 Km from North to South and 50 Km from East to West. Scheduled tribes called 'Dangies' predominantly inhabit Dang. According to the 2001 census, the total population of the district was reported to be 1, 86, 712 out of which males were 50.35 per cent and females were 49.65 per cent. 98 per cent of the total population of the district is Tribal; there are 311 villages in the district and 70 group panchayats functioning in the district.

The total number of literate reported as per 2001 census was 91, 275, out of which males were 59.56 per cent and females were 40, 44 per cent. Dang district consist of only rural schools with single block. The female literacy rate is the third lowest from amongst all the districts in the state of Gujarat. Thus, an analysis in to tribal community participation in primary education yields significant insight into the current situation of tribal community participation in primary education of Dang district. It may give idea of current status of primary education in Dang. So such a study has great practical value as it helps in improving the status of elementary education among the tribal as well as making guideline for curriculum renewal / development in education pertaining to community participation for making primary education more thorough, realistic and practical.

**Objectives of the Study**

To study the structure of different committees in the context of community participation in the elementary school activities

*Population*: All the schools of the Dang district in the year 2009-10, constitute the total population, for the present study.

*Sample*: Dang is having only one Block Resource Centre with thirty two Cluster Resource Centers. The clusters were made based on the location by District Primary Education Office and therefore, these were considered as different strata, which were considered as basis for stratification of the sample. Therefore, thirty two clusters were considered as the strata for the sample. The stratified random sample was drawn from the identified population. Accordingly school was considered as unit of sample. By using the 'paper slip and container technique' 10 per cent schools were selected randomly, from the identified strata for the sample. However, to give due consideration to maintain semblance in the proportion of the size of the sample, from each cluster one school was selected randomly and those clusters having more than fifteen schools, two schools were randomly selected. Therefore, total forty schools were selected as the sample for the present study.

*Tools*: The information schedule was prepared for the school headmaster

*Collection of data*: For the purpose of collecting data for the study, investigator had personally gone to schools constituting the sample and collected the data.

*Major Findings*: The data analysis is based on information collected through an information schedule, official records, observation schedule and interviews of the school principles.

There were total forty sampled schools and each school had constituted the VEC/MTA/PTA and VCWC committees.

- There were total forty sampled schools and each school had constituted the VEC/MTA/PTA and VCWC committees.
- Of the total schools, twenty two (55 per cent) schools had one to four VEC members, seventeen (42.5 per cent) schools had five to eight VEC members and one (2.5 per cent) school had nine to twelve VEC members in village education committee.
- It was observed that six (15 per cent) schools had no VEC agenda book while thirty four (85 per cent) schools had VEC

agenda book from that twenty seven (79.41 per cent) schools had VEC agenda book of year 2008, five (14.70 per cent) schools had VEC agenda book of year 2007 and two (5.89 per cent) schools had VEC agenda book of year 2006.

- With regard to constitution of committee in the schools, nineteen (47.50 per cent) schools committees were constituted under DPEP, six (15 per cent) schools committees were constituted after DPEP and fifteen (37.50 per cent) schools had no information regarding the year of constitution of the committees.
- The number of committee members present in meetings was ranging from three to forty members. In Five (12.50 per cent) schools date was not mentioned in the agendas written, two (5 per cent) schools without writing agendas in VEC book signature of committee members was there and one (2.50 per cent) school in all the meetings same five committee members were present.
- In twenty nine (72.5 per cent) schools all the committee members had received training, nine (22.5 per cent) schools had no information regarding the training of committee members, two (5 per cent) schools the committee members had not received any training, however all most all (92.48 per cent) of the committee members informed that they have not received any training.

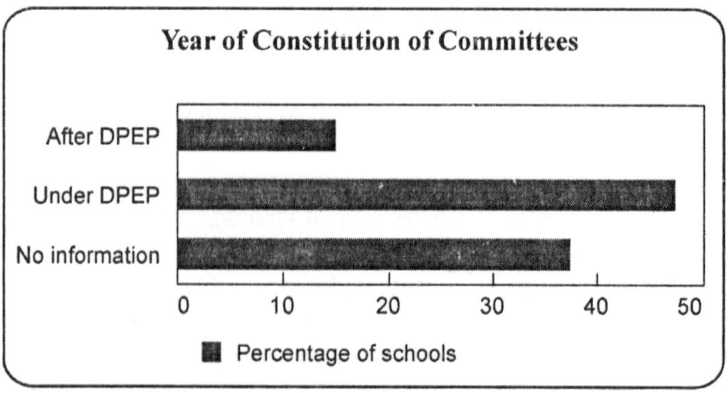


***Figure 13.1:*** *The year of the constitution of committees in the schools*

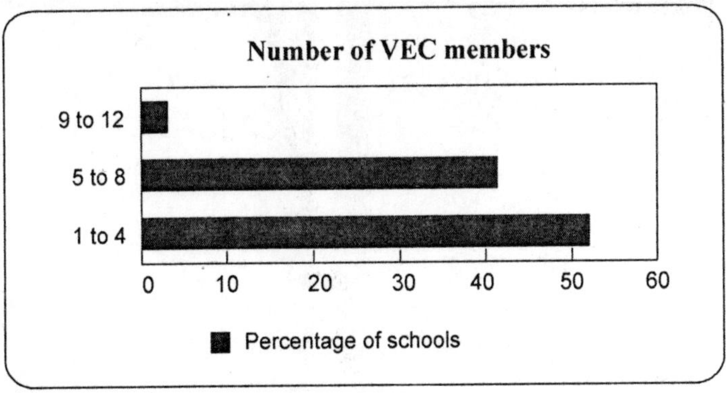


***Figure 13.2:** The number of VEC members in Village Education Committee*

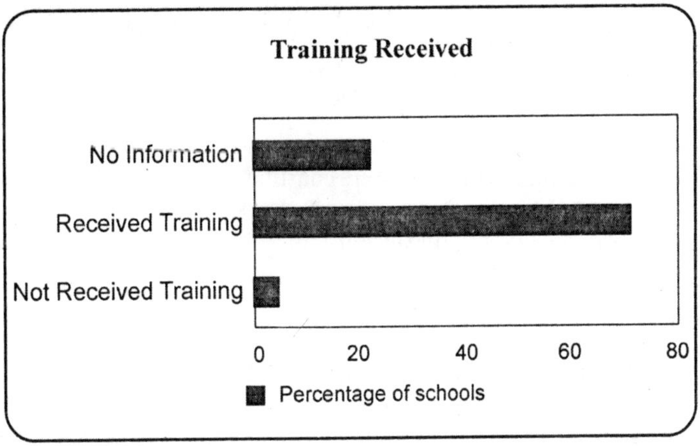


***Figure 13.3:** The training received by the committee members*

- It was observed that in most of the schools agendas were not written in detail. In thirty two (80 per cent) schools agendas were written while in two (5 per cent) schools agendas were not written.
- In four (10 per cent) schools signature of all the committee member present in meeting was there, twenty five (62.5 per cent) schools signature of all the committee members present in meeting was not there, five (12.5 per cent) schools agendas were written in VEC book but signature of committee members present in meeting was not there.

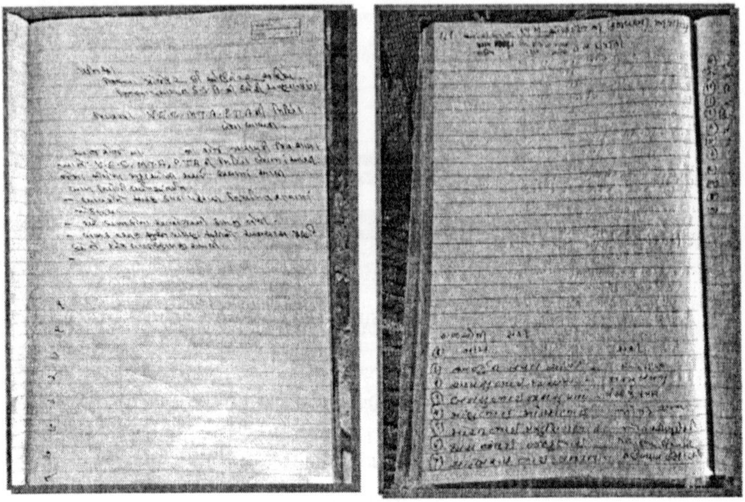

**Figure 13.4:** *VEC agenda books with no signature of members present in meeting and signature without written agenda*

With regard to structure of committees, it could be concluded that as per SSA norms committees were constituted on records but the responses of functionaries revealed the agendas made, meetings were conducted on records and grants utilized but still neither the functionaries nor the beneficiaries were aware about the basic philosophy behind community participation. The number of committee members participated in committee meetings was less. The school records showed that most of the committee members had received the training to carry out school work but committee members had reported that fewer of them had received the training. The year of constitution of the committees in sampled schools showed the wide range of differences. The observed VEC agenda books revealed that agendas were not written in detail. There were agenda books in which agendas were written but the signature of committee members were not there while on other side signature of committee members were there but agendas were not written. In most of the schools once the committees were constituted, during consecutive years the same committee kept on functioning and members remained the same. The committee members had reported that they were the members of committee for past years. Even, there were committee members, who did not know the name of committee, of which they were the members. Many functionaries were only worried to fulfill the norms set by the SSA, thus the committees were constituted to fulfill the requirement of objectives set by the SSA and do not provide the scope for involvement of tribal in the school. The constitution of committees was not by choice but by selection of head master or teachers. Group discussion and interviews with tribal revealed that neither functionaries nor the tribal were aware of the basic philosophy behind constitution of committees at the grassroots level and role of community in ensuring quality elementary education wherein community owns the school and takes care of not just the infrastructural development but also the academics of the school which includes the regularity of students as well as teachers and the all round development of the students in most of the schools. The committees were constituted and agenda books were maintained for fulfilling the norms set by the SSA but not gear up the involvement of the tribal in the elementary school activities. Therefore, both functionaries and beneficiaries require orientation, sensitization, motivation, awareness and training to work with dedication.

**Conclusion**

The study dealt with the participation of tribal of the Dangs in elementary school activities. The study revealed that committees were constituted, agendas made, grants utilized and meetings were conducted but neither functionaries nor the beneficiaries were aware with the basic philosophy behind the community participation and its role in elementary education. The meetings, training, orientation programmes and activities were organized based on guidelines given by the SSA, thus they fulfill the norms set by the SSA but do not provide opportunity for participation of tribal. The participation of tribal in committee meetings, programmes, training and other school activities was very less. The most of the teachers and head masters organized prescribed programmes and activities in the school but provide very less scope of involvement of tribal in it. The most of the functionaries were worried about the prescribed norms and thus conceal the realities of the schools.

Thus, on the basis of the study it can be concluded that prescriptive policies cannot gear up the participation of tribal, a scope for more and more participation has to be generated and tribal should be stimulated to realize their role. Unless, the tribal, both functionaries and beneficiaries will be aware with their roles and responsibility, the involvement of tribal in elementary schools could not possible. This indicates that a lot needs to be done for involvement of tribal in the elementary school activities.

## REFERENCES

Ambhasat, N. K. & Rath, K. B. (1995). 'Effect of household community and school factors on enrolment, retention and achievement among tribal students' in Buch, M. B. (edited) *Sixth Survey of Research in Education.* New Delhi: NCERT.

Banwasi Seva Ashram (1994). '*A Case Study of Banwasi Seva Ashram*' in National Meet on the role of the community in the context of UEE. New Delhi: NCERT.

Bhargava (1989). 'A study of educational facilities available in schools of tribal and non tribal districts' in Buch, M. B. (edited) *Fourth Survey of Research in Education*, New Delhi: NCERT.

Das, A. (1991). 'Innovative education in remote tribal blocks: A search for contents and methods, Independent study' in Buch, M. B. (edited) *Fifth Survey of Research in Education*. New Delhi: NCERT.

Ekka, E. M. (1990). '*Development of tribal education in Orissa after Independence*', Ph.D., in Buch, M. B. (edited) *Fifth Survey of Research in Education*, New Delhi: NCERT.

Epstein, J., Lucretia, C., Karen, C., Mavis, G. and Beth, S. (1997). "School, family and community partnership: Your Handbook for Action". ERIC: ED Printers.

Gandhi Vidyapith (2004). *A case study of Gandhi Vidyapith*. In National Meet on the role of the community in the context of UEE, New Delhi, NCERT.

Kumar, S., Patel, R. C. & Mehta, A. K. (1999). Community participation in primary education. *The Primary Teacher*, Oct, pp. 33-41.

Panda, B. K. (1995). 'A study of functions, organization and impact of the tribal schools in Koraput district of Orissa' in Buch, M. B. (edited) *Sixth Survey of Research in Education*. New Delhi:NCERT.

Panigrahi, S. C. (1992). A study of educational development of tribals in Kalakhadi district of Orissa, Unpublished Ph.D. thesis, C.A.S.E., M.S.U., Vadodara.

Raman, G. V. (1989). 'Problems of education among the tribal communities of Andhra Pradesh: A case study of Ashram schools' Ph.D. in Buch, M. B. (edited) *Fifth Survey of Research in Education*. New Delhi: NCERT.

Rao, G. K. (1999). "A study of the relationship between community participation and school effectiveness" in studies on learning organization, community participation and school effectiveness at primary stage: International Perspective. New Delhi; NCERT.

Roy, J. J. (1995). 'A study of innovative practices to ensure school effectiveness among deprived groups' in Buch, M. B. (edited) *Fourth Survey of Research in Education*. New Delhi; NCERT.

Sahoo (2004). *A study of participation of tribals in primary education*. In National Seminar on Effective management of Primary Education, Vadodara, M.S.U.

Sathyabalan, V. (1993) Effectiveness of primary education in rural areas of Tamil Nadu, Unpublished Ph. D. thesis, C.A.S.E., M.S.U., Vadodara.

Wilson, M. J. (1997). 'A study on impact of participation of the tribal community in the growth and development of school management in the tribal areas of Vishakhapatnam district', Ph. D. in Buch, M. B. (edited) *Sixth Survey of Research in Education*. New Delhi: NCERT.

# Contributors

**A, Mary Bini,** Assistant Professor, Regional Institute of Education (RIE), Bhopal, Madhya Pradesh

**Agnihotri, Ashish**, Ph.D. Research Scholar, Academy of International Studies, Jamia Millia Islamia (Central University) New Delhi-1100025

**Amin, Jyotsna Ashok (Dr.)**, Assistant Professor, Department of Education [CASE], Faculty of Education and Psychology, The Maharaja Sayajirao University of Baroda, Vadodara- 390002

**Bhaskar, Shilpi**, M.Phil. Research Scholar, National University of Educational Planning and Administration (NUEPA), New Delhi-110016

**Bist, Swati**, Ph.D. Research Scholar, Department of Social Work, Jamia Millia Islamia (Central University), New Delhi-1100025

**Chaudhari, Priti (Dr.)**, Assistant Professor, Department of Education [CASE], Faculty of Education and Psychology, The Maharaja Sayajirao University of Baroda, Vadodara- 390002

**Chennat, Sailaja (Dr.)**, Associate Professor, CIE, Department of Education, University of Delhi, Delhi-110007

**Chowdhary, Vertika**, M.Phil. Research Scholar, CIE, Department of Education, University of Delhi, Delhi-110007

**Das, Pankaj**, NCERT Doctoral Fellow, CIE, Department of Education, University of Delhi, Delhi-110007

**Lakra, Abhineet Kala**, Ph.D. Research Scholar, Zakir Husain Centre for Educational Studies, School of Social Sciences, Jawaharlal Nehru University (JNU), New Delhi-110067

**Mishra, Prabuddh Kumar**, Assistant Professor, Regional Institute of Education (RIE), Bhopal, Madhya Pradesh

**Narula, Manju (Dr.)**, Assistant Professor, Department of Educational Administration, National University of Educational Planning and Administration (NUEPA), New Delhi-110016

**Padhi, Sambit Kumar (Dr.)**, Assistant Professor, Department of Education, Guru Ghasidas Vishwavidyalaya, Bilaspur, Chhattisgarh

**Paul, Rupashree**, ICSSR Doctoral Fellow, Department of Education, Assam University, Silchar-788011

**Patel, R.C (Dr.)**, Reader, Department of Education [CASE], Faculty of Education and Psychology, The Maharaja Sayajirao University of Baroda, Vadodara-390002

**Purkayastha**, Bornita. Assistant Professor, Department of Education, D.D.M. (Govt.) College, Khowai, Tripura-799201

**Sagarika, Sipra**, M.Phil. Research Scholar, Centre for Study of Social System, School of Social Sciences, Jawaharlal Nehru University (JNU), New Delhi-110067